Bonfire of the Humanities

The Television Series
Robert Thompson, *Series Editor*

Syracuse University Press is pleased to announce its new *Television Series* with the publication of David Marc's *Bonfire of the Humanities*.

The series will provide readers with critical studies about popular TV as a creative and artistic medium. Television and TV programming, an area underexplored until now, will be one of the major focuses. Stories about the creators, producers, directors, and writers are planned, and the series will reprint classic works and texts recommended by scholars and others in the field. The series editor is Professor Robert Thompson, who teaches at the S. I. Newhouse School of Public Communications at Syracuse University.

BONFIRE

OF THE

HUMANITIES

Television, Subliteracy,
and Long-Term Memory Loss

David Marc

Foreword by Susan J. Douglas
Illustrations by Heinz Emigholz

Syracuse University Press

The eight drawings in this book are from the series *The Basis of Make-Up* by
Heinz Emigholz. Permission by the artist to reprint them is gratefully acknowledged.

The paper used in this publication meets the minimum requirements of American
National Standard for Information Sciences—Permanence of Paper for
Printed Library Materials, ANSI Z39.48-1984. ∞™

Library of Congress Cataloging-in-Publication Data
Marc, David.
    Bonfire of the humanities : television, subliteracy, and long-term
memory loss / David Marc ; foreword by Susan Douglas.
      p. cm. — (The Television series)
    Includes bibliographical references and index.
    ISBN 0-8156-0321-5
    1. Television broadcasting—Social aspects—United States.
2. Television broadcasting—United States—Influence. 3. Literacy—
United States. 4. Popular culture—United States. I. Title.
II. Series.
PN1992.6.M366   1995
302.23'45'0973—dc20   94-48616

Manufactured in the United States of America

For my teachers,
Sherman Paul, Milton Kessler, and Ken Jacobs

David Marc is the author of *Demographic Vistas: Television in American Culture*, *Comic Visions: Television Comedy and American Culture*, and coauthor of *Prime Time, Prime Movers*. He has taught communications, writing, television, film, and literature at the Annenberg School for Communication, University of Southern California; UCLA; University of California, San Diego; California Institute of Technology; Brandeis University; and Brown University.

Answer: Mnemosyne, the Goddess of Memory, is their mother.
Question: Who are the Muses?

Jeopardy clue, 29 January 1994

Contents

Illustrations

Foreword

Susan J. Douglas

David Marc is on a tear and nothing—not the National Endowment for the Humanities, college reading lists, political correctness, televangelists, or the culture industry—is safe. Marc is outraged, and frightened, that the humanities—as a collection of disciplines and as a way of shaping our apprehension of the world and our place in it—are going down in flames. And while he cites the usual suspects—television, consumerism, careerism, and the vocationalizing of undergraduate education—he also blames all of us, whether on the left, the right, or in the middle, who claim to practice the humanities and who think we are preventing their extinction.

As a result, there is much to infuriate the reader in the following pages. At least, *I* got infuriated. But I also laughed out loud, and I underlined and starred passages that ring all too true. It helps that Marc is a sensational writer, and that he is deeply concerned with what distresses many of us: the crisis of literacy in the face of an ever-encroaching ever-centralized, and ever-powerful electronic media system that has deeply compromised not just the humanities but our entire educational system. And Marc is in a particularly interesting position to write the tirade that follows. He is an academic who loves poetry, literature, philosophy, history, and writing. He believes that reading great books and learning to write stylish prose matter deeply, not just for one's future career, but, more importantly, for one's ability to live a meaningful life. But Marc is a baby boomer too, bona fide member of the first television generation who made his reputation as a television critic, and he appreciates all too well the pulsing seductions and blandishments of the electronic media. In the face of the current crisis, where is a guy like this left to stand?

There is a great deal of irony in these essays, not the least of which is the way they are organized and titled. Each essay, which bemoans the increasing irrelevance of literacy and the progressive shrinkage of the American attention span in the face of television, is called a "segment," so we are given permission to read around, to not necessarily start at the beginning, but to chapter surf if we so wish. In "Segment Two," Marc writes passionately and poignantly about our inability to reconcile our national reverence for literacy—meaning reading books and writing on paper—with the reality of how information is stored and used in this electronic age. College teachers have it so tough when marking papers, notes Marc, because we are charged with inflating and celebrating the value of literacy in a society where real literacy, in all its forms, matters less and less.

There are hilarious stories here and elsewhere about conversations with undergraduates who know they have to jump through the reading and writing hoops in ways they may never have to again. Even if they can't articulate it, notes Marc, students grasp the culture's enormous contradictions—hypocrisy, even—about the importance of literacy in every day life and work. We in the humanities, Marc insists, have failed to confront adequately the widening gap between "the stated aims of American education and demonstrated needs of American society." Skill with the written word is celebrated while at the same time our culture exhibits "an almost universal indifference to bad writing." And too many academic humanists get on their high-culture horse about the banality of television and corruptions of rock music (yes, Allan Bloom comes in for a pasting here as a "redneck humanist"), while failing to come to terms with the consciousness-altering effects of the mass media as a system of knowledge. "Segment Three" continues this theme by focusing on the corporate construction of memory, and here Marc urges us to reread Hans Magnus Enzenberger's prescient analysis of the culture industry's increasing monopoly in collective memory distribution. The incessant rewriting of history by the mass media into false, sepia-toned tintypes of consensus from below and beneficence from above corrupts not just our real history but the very notions of history and memory themselves.

By now, you may want to know more about Marc the person, and the first segment combines autobiography, cultural history, and more tales out of school about the incredibly petty depths to which academic humanists can sink when they look inward instead of outward and obsess about idiotic institutional politics instead of on the national intel-lectual crisis that threatens us all. In one of my favorite segments, the fifth, Marc provides his version of the rise of television criticism in the academy and reclaims the brilliant critic Gilbert Seldes from the remainder bin of media studies. Throughout his life, Seldes was a rare breed, an intellectual who appreciated, early on, popular arts that more snobbish types dismissed as vulgar yet inconsequential. He understood completely the importance of jazz in the 1920s when other white critics dismissed it as primitive, corrupting jungle music, and he took television seriously when the "mass culture" critics tried to deepen the moat between the "high arts" and the more lowly "popular arts."

"Culture Without Content," a.k.a. segment four, is Marc's own take on political correctness. Here I found myself writing "yes, but . . ." in the margins one minute and an emphatic "yes!!" the next. Marc can be incendiary here, but his concern that political correctness has enforced self-censorship among many, to the detriment of the very spirit of the humanities, is a concern we can't afford to ignore. Possibly the funniest and most free-ranging segment is the sixth, which offers a great reading of the significance of the yuppie as an archetype, as well as some thoughts on cars, Marshall McLuhan, and literature. And finally, in the last module, Marc notes shrewdly that televangelists, who make their billions denouncing the godlessness of an overly materialistic consumer society, can't possibly promote their brand of religion on TV without automatically promoting consumerism itself.

Those who have seen humanities departments, programs, courses, and faculty cut at a variety of institutions will find Marc's take on this situation bracing and thought-provoking. For Marc sees the mass media, and television in particular, as both a cause and a symptom of this major epistemological shift—and crisis. Concerns about the dumbing of America and the loss of "cultural literacy" in the face of a national media-induced trance have escalated since the 1980s. But Marc does not focus on the familiar targets, ethnic and racial minorities and an economic and intellectual underclass.

Instead, Marc asks us to look in the mirror. He urges us to move beyond two knee-jerk reactions to television: either to denounce it as inferior trash "we" never watch (except for *Masterpiece Theater*) or to rush to fill our syllabi with films and videos as a way to reach our visually oriented students. In contemplating the future of the humanities, of literacy, of public and private memory, Marc asks academic humanists to come to terms—especially in their teaching—with this enormous epistemological sea change we are all experiencing and bemoaning. That means analyzing how the electronic media, for better and worse, are reshaping the role of higher education for the next century. It means asking our students and ourselves to look outward rather than inward and to think in much broader terms about what happens to a culture when two ways of apprehending the world, one based on reading and writing, the other on consuming the offerings of the mass media, both collide and overlap. Marc often suggests that the bonfire consuming the humanities is now already burning out of control and probably can't be put out. He may be right. The final answer lies with us, our students, and our willingness to engage with society at large as political, public, activist intellectuals.

Acknowledgments

The following contributions to this book are gratefully acknowledged: to Daniel J. Czitrom for giving this book its title; to David Zakon for providing reference assistance; and to Daniel J. Barnett for his surgical encouragement.

Permission from publishers to use or reprint material in this book is also acknowledged.

Parts of this book appeared in the column, "Annals of the Death of the Humanities," which ran in *The Boston Review* during 1989 and 1990.

"Mass Memory: The Past in the Age of Television," originally appeared in a slightly different form in *Rhetorical Memory and Delivery: Classical Concepts for Contemporary Composition* (1993) edited by J. Fred Reynolds. It appears by permission of the publisher, Lawrence Erlbaum Associates, Inc.

"The Emergence of Television Criticism, 1920–1988," appeared in a slightly different form in "Mass Culture, Class Culture, Democracy, and Prime-Time: Television Criticism and the Question of Quality" in *Meanings of the Medium: Perspectives on the Art of Television* (1990) edited by Katherine Usher Henderson and Joseph Anthony Mazzeo. It appears by permission of the publisher, Praeger/Greenwood Publishing Group.

A portion of Chapter Seven originally appeared in *The Philadelphia Inquirer* (2 May 1994).

Bonfire of the Humanities

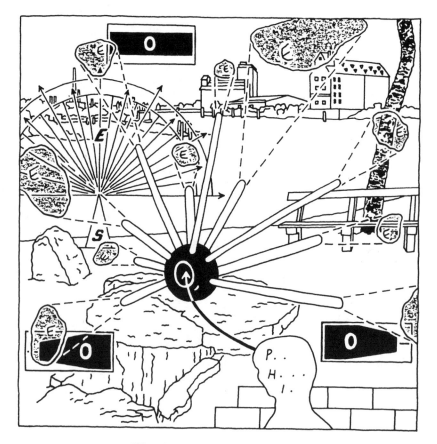

"Happiness must remain an issue."

Introduction

According to a report delivered to Congress by the National Endowment for the Humanities (NEH) during the final year of the Reagan administration, Americans during the 1970s spent twice as much on admissions to spectator sports as they did on admissions to cultural events. So, what else is new? This: by the late 1980s, that situation had been completely reversed. The leisure-time culture dollar had not only caught up with the sports buck, but had eclipsed it by almost 10 percent. What's that you say? Could it be? Greek revival? A new constitution for the republic of mass culture? A happy future for *les beaux arts* in the land of Coca-Cola? Cool your jets, muse-worshippers. The Endowment's report was, on balance, "mixed."

During roughly the same two decades that art was jogging past sport toward the box-office finish line, the number of students majoring in humanities subjects at U.S. colleges and universities was dropping by over 30 percent, despite the fact that the total number of bachelor degrees awarded was doubling. In a clinical assessment of the situation, Frank Rhodes, the president of Cornell University, observed that "traditional liberal arts courses have lost much of their ability to exert a transforming and enriching influence on students of humanity, and the humanities have become unattractive."[1] Unattractive? Dr. Rhodes, you are a diplomat. Furthermore the unmistakable lack of interest shown by students for these homely subjects has been reflected gradually in a lack of institutional support for them. With tuition prices what they are, the customer is always right.

It is now possible to enter the room as a college graduate in these United States without ever having taken a history course (37 percent of accredited schools do not require one), without ever having taken philosophy (62 percent will let that one slide), and without ever having studied a foreign language (a whopping 77 percent have stopped plagu-

3

ing degree candidates with that mumbo-jumbo). "You have students going to college who don't know what the humanities are and who may never find out," concluded National Endowment Chair Lynne V. Cheney.[2]

There are at least two substantial issues conjured by these statistics. One is the loss of credibility that the humanities have been suffering in general since Marx, Freud, Darwin, and other shapers of contemporary intellectual consciousness started declaring their studies of such subjects as political economy, sexual desire, and the origin of human existence to be "scientific" in nature. Attempting to free themselves from the web of religious mysticism that protected these areas of inquiry from rational scrutiny, self-consciously forward-looking nineteenth-century thinkers adopted the jargon of scientific method as a justification—and as a flag —of their progressive defiance of traditional taboos. A century later, that well-intentioned impulse seems like a corny rhetorical ploy. "Scientific socialism" has thus far turned out to be an oxymoron that has done little to rattle the great chain of being; psychoanalysis is a crapshoot (and at a 150 bucks an hour, a rather high-stakes game for most neurotics), and evolution remains a theory. But the damage has been done. If information ain't science, or at least dressed up for the lab, it's "just your opinion," a sarcastic put-down in a culture dominated by Pavlovian marketing theories. Even fans of Adam and Eve feel compelled to promote their version of the origin of species as creation*ism*.

Another issue raised by the NEH's report on the demise of the humanities is somewhat narrower in terms of epic sweep but no less important for the future of thinking. How can increasing public interest in the arts be squared with decreasing public interest in formal study of the history and appreciation of the arts? Isn't Culture a culture? *New York Times* education reporter Edward B. Fiske offers a plausible explanation to this enigma. Fiske berates professional humanists for their recent reluctance to apply their thinking to the "fundamental questions." He notes, for example, that "most major philosophy departments are dominated by analytic types who are more interested in examining language than in raising questions about the meaning of life."[3] The accusation implicit in Fiske's remark recalls Walt Whitman's challenge to the parlor-roomism of nineteenth-century American scholars: "Have you studied so long just to get at the meaning of poems?"

Dr. Rhodes agrees: "Many of those who profess to be humanists devote their lives to areas of high abstraction, decoding texts and deconstructing poems while the larger issues of the world and humankind's place in it elude them. With notable and commendable exceptions, humanists are not demonstrably more wise, more committed, more human than their neighbors." Well, maybe Dr. Rhodes is not such a diplomat after all.

Frankly this thinly veiled tweak at deconstructionism from far above Cayuga's waters is not nearly punishment enough for those bastards. By "freeing the text from history" the decons did a good job during the 1980s of turning the study of culture into a kind of mental aerobics session, where the furiousness of running in place is valued over getting anywhere. Though I still find myself amazed each time this happens, it is not uncommon during this evil, gray period of post-deconstructionist malaise for students in my literature, film, and television classes to ask me whether or not they are "allowed" to include "personal opinion" in their papers.

"What else would you write about?" I ask them, affecting what I've come to think of as my own special brand of pre-postmodern naïveté about the question.

They become impatient, as if I am trying to trick them. "Are we supposed to say what we think the book means, or are we supposed to do a research paper on it?"

"But this is a novel . . . how would you . . ."

"Professor So-and-So takes off credit for personal opinion. Do you?"

"Only if it is banal, morally bankrupt, or without basis in the text."

Exasperation mounts. Doesn't this guy know that a "B" in this course could keep me out of law school?

If the NEH statistics are correct, a remarkable number of people are resisting the attempts of their teachers to make them hate art. They are graduating from college and going to theaters, museums, concert halls, libraries, and highcult cable channels in increasing numbers, having successfully avoided the casuistry of message doctors who attempt to hold the erotic powers of human imagination the hostage of ideologically motivated classroom theory. Or, as Mr. Fiske succinctly put it, "It should come as no surprise that the public is looking beyond the academic environment to satisfy its craving for culture."[4]

Indeed, beyond the academic environment, the humanities major, member of a dying breed, wanders out into the fin de siècle mall of consumer culture bearing the mark of Cain. It is already a cliché of American family economics to pity the poor parents who have learned that their child has risked membership in the bourgeoisie—perhaps risked the possibility of ever becoming solvent—by majoring in English or art history, courses of study that will run you the same fifty-to-a-hundred grand as chemistry or accounting. What can mom and pop do but curse the brashness of youth, continue to fill out Parents' Confidential Statements, and say a prayer for professional graduate school?

Of all the industrial folklore cataloging the degradation of the humanities, one tale in particular, casually reported in the press, remains a favorite because it cuts like a Ginsu knife directly into the heart of the matter: In the winter of 1988, the credit card division of Citibank, largest banking institution in the United States, set up a table on the campus of the University of California at Berkeley for the purpose of signing up graduating seniors to become recipients of freshly minted Mastercards and Visas. A sign on the table announced "no previous credit history required," in effect promising that, as graduates of one of the nation's leading universities, applicants would be awarded their passports to overconsumption without so much as the usual audit of credit history. Citibank had been making such offers at selected "better" colleges since the mid-1980s.

An inconsistency emerged, however, between Citibank's sales pitch and its practices. There turned out to be one bit of "credit history" a responsible financial institution simply could not ignore. According to the *Los Angeles Times,* "the bank routinely rejected students who listed majors in the humanities, such as English, history or art. The bank's basic rationale is that these students are less likely to repay debts because they will not land the high-paying jobs that go to business or engineering graduates."[5]

Although the old boys and young women who dominate the faculty clubs these days may be morally outraged, ethically shocked, and so on by such blatant discrimination, apparently the bank's policy did not strike many students as anything unusual. It only hit the media loop when Mr. Kennedy Yip, a Berkeley student who had been majoring in mathematics, and who already had a Citibank Visa card, switched his major to rhetoric and subsequently applied for a Citibank Mastercard. Qualifying as a graduating senior, and having paid all his previous Visa bills to boot, Mr. Yip believed he had every reason to expect routine approval of his application for a Mastercard. This proved to be an innocent assumption for a person who had traded in his calculator for the second-class citizenship of language study.

On 13 February 1988, he received a letter from Citibank explaining that he had been turned down because of his "field of study." When he consulted with friends about the situation, Mr. Yip reported, he was advised to apply again and "fake my major as business administration or engineering . . . lots of students lie about their majors." But Mr. Yip, perhaps in the spirit of his new major, balked at this suggestion and instead chose to stick to the truth and protest.

Do humanities students have legal recourse against such blatant discrimination? No, according to Professor Edwin L. Rubin of the Berkeley Law School. The law prohibits using race or sex in deciding matters of credit; devotees of art, literature, history, and philosophy enjoy no such protections. "In the absence of a credit history, we look at field of study as one indicator of an individual's ability to repay debt," explained Citibank official Bill McGuire. Another bank spokesperson characterized the story as a publicity "nightmare," a factor—apparently the sole factor—that led the bank's parent body, Citicorp, to go against its unimpeded business judgment and issue a statement about "phasing out" the antihumanities policy.

And so, these two newspaper articles and some snide commentary concerning them aside, what is this book about? We—you and I, reader and writer—have borne witness to what may be called, with a deft tongue, the "de-epistemologicalization of the humanities," a historical process whose origins can be traced to eighteenth-century Cartesian scientism. Over the last two hundred years, empiricism has so utterly eclipsed intuitive, imaginative sensibility as a salient standard of truth in Western civilization that the humanities, to the degree that they are still cultivated at all, are treated as a kind of quaint, antiquarian ornament to "real" thinking. Appreciation of the arts, literature, history, or philosophy may upon occasion be trotted out to lend genteel status to a self-conscious individual or institution, but these disciplines have otherwise been eighty-sixed as tools essential to the getting of knowledge for the purpose of making rational decisions.

As a result, the informed imaginative synthesis of heart and mind— the process that is the very foundation of humanistic thinking—withers to the status of voodoo. Or worse yet, it finds its real powers eroded by the acids of a phony scientism, as if the appreciation of a poem or a painting could be axiomatic. Actual science—the use of the empirical method to discover the physical, chemical, and biological properties of the universe—is not a threat to the humanities, but rather an essential complement to subjective understanding. Damage occurs when the rhetoric of science is conjured to "give teeth" to critical judgment, as if the cloaking of an individual's unique perceptions in empirical robes will somehow bestow legitimacy upon ideas that might otherwise be construed as "just somebody's opinion." Under such conditions, the vitality of the imagination decays as it is transformed into a bad imitation of scientific method.

The dumping of an entire epistemology by a civilization is by no means an overnight event. In the United States it is being accomplished mostly at universities and grant-giving foundations by gradual accretions. The literary offerings of an English department are diminished as the department is required to teach more writing "service" courses without any increase in budget. A classics course retires along with its teacher while whole new departments of computer science are added to the curriculum. And grants for research in "Audience Effects Methodology" and "Media Ecology" are established to study television, while language departments refuse (or are refused) the opportunity to study the fate of language in the paths that it is now traveling.

It is particularly daunting and dangerous that the humanities have fallen on such hard times just at a moment in history when technological breakthroughs have extended verbal and visual expression—especially drama and information about current events (i.e., rhetoric)—to such a wide circle of society at large. Wasn't a humanities-based liberal arts education once thought to be the foundation of a democratic society that invited the engagement of its citizens with the political and social dilemmas that affect their lives? One of the reasons that so much of television has stunk, stinks, and will stink is that the corporate owners of the medium and their customers have insisted that they are involved primarily in a social science experiment rather than an artistic venture, and that most humanist critics have accommodated this lie by looking the other way to flatter their own gentility. For example, the small amount of agitation for "better" television in the early 1950s, as the medium was cutting its teeth, came not from scholars but from a small group of newspaper reviewers, including John Crosby of the *New York Herald Tribune* and Jack Gould of the *New York Times*.

In 1948, the year of Milton Berle's Tuesday night breakthrough, Robert Warshow wrote, "The sense of tragedy is a luxury of aristocratic societies, [in which] the fate of the individual is not conceived of as having a direct and legitimate political importance, being determined [instead] by a fixed and supra-political—that is, non-controversial—moral order or fate. Modern equalitarian societies, however, . . . always base themselves on the claim that they are making life happier; the avowed function of the modern state, at least in its ultimate terms, is not only to regulate social relations, but also to determine the quality and the possibilities of human life in general. Happiness thus becomes the chief political issue—in a sense, the only political issue—and for that reason it can never be treated as an issue at all."[6]

Murder, rape, child abuse; deodorant, sneakers, hamburger. Racism, sexism, homophobia; Mercedes, Armani, Rolex. The wave of terror; the wash of marketing. Is this any way to live? Television is the stage upon which the public drama is enacted. The public drama is the common reference point by which society continuously recreates itself. Happiness must remain a issue.

1. Edward B. Fiske, *New York Times*, 5 Oct. 1988, B12.
2. Ibid.
3. Ibid.
4. Ibid.
5. *Los Angeles Times*, 12 March 1988, D2.
6. Robert Warshow, *The Immediate Experience* (New York: Doubleday, 1962), 127.

"Would you rather be watching TV than reading this book?"

Chosen By Television
A Viewer in the City

Q.: What is an American intellectual?
A.: Someone who watches PBS and listens to NPR.
Q.: What is an American bohemian intellectual?
A.: Someone who watches PBS and listens to NPR but doesn't subscribe.

Sherman Paul, the most passionately literate person I ever met, used to make a point of telling me that all critical writing is autobiography. The "method" dictated by this belief was—and remains—something less than à la mode. Meet the work. Allow the visceral reaction to take place. Seek the historical circumstances of period, medium, and genre. Find quiet. Listen to yourself respond. Record the experience. No need to erect a theory to stand between you and the expression of another human being; there's already enough crap dividing us. No need to follow the theories of a Nazi bigamist.

Perhaps because Sherm loved reading so fully, he never displayed the book fetish that so many lit. profs. advertise to highlight the elevation of their brows. Literature is part of culture; not the other way around. As its radical meaning in biology suggests, a culture is a source of nutrition for growth—in this case growth of consciousness, the personal and the social always in synthesis. A conscientious teacher, Sherm not only allowed me, but urged me, to locate and explore the *ecos* of whatever mythic wellspring had nourished me. If the source proved to be hopelessly polluted, all the more urgency for scrupulous examination and rehabilitation. I got my education from three middle-aged Jewish men, all married . . . with children: Sherman Paul, a Brahmin critic with a dozen books published and a Harvard Ph.D.; Ken Jacobs, an optical illusionist and college professor who was thrown out of high school; and Milton Kessler, a poet who schlepped the baggage of diaspora culture across the twentieth century with a quite unusual grace. All deeply suspicious of answers, they seemed to be asking the same question: Is the world a propitious place for the self?

I was born in April 1951, a little less than five months before the premier of *I Love Lucy*. Harry Truman was president. Telephones were black and could not be detached from the wall by technocratic laity. If no one was home, those heavy little desk models just kept ringing, perhaps even "ringing off the hook," as the old predigital expression used to go. There were neither video stores nor VCRs as videotape did not yet exist. Ditto for FAX machines, retail copy shops, home computers, or computers that could fit in homes. Antennae dominated the squat skyline of Borough Park, an otherwise obscure Brooklyn neighborhood that was the staging area for the developing psychologies of such estimable American personalities as Sandy Koufax, Buddy Hackett, and Alan Dershowitz.

My family already owned a TV set, a formidable piece of furniture that overpowered the living room of our rent-controlled apartment. It played most of the day and all through prime time, though at this cusp in the evolution of mass communication systems a radio still ruled my mother's kitchen while she cooked and even baked. My favorite shows included *Father Knows Best, Sea Hunt,* and *Have Gun, Will Travel.* In retrospect the fact that my father was dead, there was no place to swim, and I'd never ridden a horse were plausible catalysts in forming my viewer loyalties.

What I could see on TV was a picture radically distinct from the vista offered by my fourth-story window: a grocery store, an empty lot, and crowds of people, many of them unreconstructed Hasidim and Sicilians, rushing down the block to and from the elevated subway. Approximately once a year the TV set would go dead and we would have to wait, sometimes as much as twenty-four hours, for a TV repairman to come and replace one or more tubes. Several times the set actually had to be removed from the apartment for some incomprehensible procedure at the appliance store. This induced a kind of chaos in our home, which sent us all scattering to the neighbors. We eventually got a second set, a portable, but that's another story.

It wasn't until more than twenty years later, sometime during Nixon's aborted second term, that I began writing about television. I had moved across New York State from Brooklyn to Binghamton, where I was studying literature at the state university, specializing in British romantic poetry, doing the grad school cha-cha-cha, alternately striving and drifting in the direction of a doctorate in English, making believe I was a Bohemian, taking long baths in the morning while listening to 1920s jazz and 1960s LSD records, paying rent with the scraps of a freshman writing program, and, to be honest, watching relatively little television compared to any other time in my life.

Binghamton, a small city still reeling from the effects of the Panic of 1872, never mind 1929, was in most ways an unselfconscious technological backwater. Apartments in this lake-effect snowbelt burg were typically heated with bizarre electrical or gas space-heating contraptions, the kind that made fire insurance out of the question. The county transit authority's bus fleet was dominated by a ramshackle collection of second-hand, discontinued models. But owing to its peculiar geographical position at the bottom of a severe depression surrounding the confluence of the Chenango and Susquehanna Rivers, Binghamton had gotten cable TV in the early 1950s, the alternative being just about no TV at all. Thus, while the citizens of the capitals of the world, from New York and Los Angeles to Tokyo and London, still struggled to manipulate their pathetic antennae, Binghamtonians had been feasting on HBO since the day it went on the air in 1972.

But I was having none of that for the moment. Instead I was engaged in a struggle with the liberal viewing habits I had enjoyed as a child. As part of the process of my civilization, I had bought into the strict line promoted by my German Jewish-American and WASP college professors that TV was actually a devilish social science experiment relentlessly conducted by Madison Avenue anti-artists and their comrades in lab coats on behalf of the Fortune 500. This view was held despite any apparent potential TV might have had as a medium for the presentation of drama, information, or other audiovisual experiences to the long-suffering peoples of the world. To watch TV was to be a lamb too eager for the slaughter of self. There was no need to say anything more about it, except for an occasional smug remark concerning the ugly little screen's stupidity, banality, sterility, or hollowness. I had an eight-inch, black-and-white portable, purchased at K-Mart, which I kept on the floor and even stashed in the closet when entertaining certain guests.

Intimidated and thus indoctrinated, I undertook to turn my back on the thousands of hours I had spent watching TV in Brooklyn, hoping to at last grow up (and fit in) by studying the mind of England. My self-satisfaction at being able to follow Elizabethan prose was growing into a frenetic appreciation of Shakespeare. Swift was making me laugh out loud. It could take me pages to tire of Pope's heroic couplets. I found myself particularly devoted to Coleridge's druggy fantasy poems, especially "This Lime Tree Bower, My Prison" and "Kubla Khan." Jane Austen was teaching me proper manners for strawberry-picking expeditions. No novelist could touch E. M. Forster, though I was disturbed—in retrospect mentally disturbed—by his at times fierce critique of the empire. And yet, as ready as I was to make myself an intellectual running dog of British cultural imperialism, I could never quite escape the native roots I had put down in front of a television set. Why did I even want to *think* about TV with the path so clear before me? The stained fabric of my couch just might be fertile American soil.

Certainly there were video demons to exorcise from a child's life of viewing: the crazy puppets, especially Mr. Bluster from *Howdy Doody;* the Three Stooges, especially Curley (I cared nothing for Shemp); the mice streaming out of everywhere on Farmer Gray cartoons; the same recurring shot of the delirious audience on *Andy's Gang;* any sitcom episode based on keeping a surprise birthday party secret from the main character; Kookie on *77 Sunset Strip.* Lacking money for a shrink or inclination for a priest, it gradually dawned on me that I had little choice but to try to invent some sort of self-help therapy to get myself free of all this nutty stuff that was clogging my attic, or was it my basement?

I wanted to be a writer, mainly because it was the only thing that I could get praise for, and that being the case, writing about TV seemed like an appropriate strategy. If the first problem in writing is locating energy, I was finding that the rediscovery of the world made possible by literature was mediating a sufficient perspective on language/storytelling to allow me to bump into distinctions between the TV-fed artifices of my Piaget years and a larger picture of things that might be called nature. TV insisted upon the punishment of evil and the rewarding of good. Thomas Hardy insisted it was as likely to be the other way around. TV emphasized that the world was a great place. Camus emphasized that it was not. TV painted a picture of laughing, happy people whose lives were filled with the unflagging love of those around them. Samuel Beckett sketched portraits of stark emptinesses dominated by nothing except, possibly, an anticipation of death, which might be a release or at least some kind of a change. I dwelled in the crevices separating these worldviews, simultaneously amused by the innocence of the devil and faithful to the catastrophic visions of the angels.

Despite all the satisfactions of reading pedigreed books and the pedigreed things that were written about them, I was terribly disappointed at how distantly literature lingered from public concern. Instant communication was turning the world into a big, never-ending soap opera of war, business, celebrity, and natural disaster, constantly evolving in the living room, on the car radio, in the morning paper. Why was literature, with all its power over me, so absent from the story? I had a notion that each book, like some mountain climbed, was bringing me closer to a benighted Xanadu of *Kultur*. But where might that place be? Under the fluorescent lights of a college classroom? At the bad-wine-and-cheese receptions following poetry readings? Tucked between the pages of the books themselves, lodged in the tiny spaces between black ink and white paper?

At the same time no searching was necessary for the culture of television. It found me wherever I hid. What was on last night, last week, last year, and last decade was subject to discussion everywhere by everyone: on the check-out line at the supermarket, on the wood-grain benches beneath the ersatz trees at the brand new malls, in the as yet unfashionable locker room at the gym. To bring ideas developed in literary study to bear on TV seemed like an urgent, noble, and even self-sacrificial idea. As it turns out, I had to settle for one out of three.

I quickly learned that the great personal disadvantage to studying American TV, as opposed to, say, British poetry, French painting, Scandinavian cinema, or Japanese flower-arranging, is that so little of the subject matter is aesthetically or intellectually satisfying in any traditional sense. Most poems and paintings and films and flower arrangements are, after all, just as bad as most TV shows. The good stuff, by definition, can never be more than a tiny fragment of the whole. De Tocqueville is compelled to point this out repeatedly in *Democracy in America;* it was his special way of pining for the ancien régime. The best works of the older arts have been savored and saved; they've weathered tests of time and trend. But TV is so new—just fifty years out of the laboratory—that quite frankly no one quite knows how to know what the good stuff is, or what it is going to be. The definable pleasures of "mastering" a work, of understanding how its expressed emotions and ideas bring its form into germinating dialogue with the historical concerns of moment and place (not to mention eternity and universe) are tough to extract from television shows. Generally speaking, on TV clarity is valued over deftness; flow over causality; resolution over catharsis. There is no, "By George, I've got it and it brings me an inch closer to being educated, civilized, and knowing the secrets of the ages!" TV is mostly just a lot of "Yeah, yeah, yeah . . . so . . ."

And yet people, lots of people, mind-boggling masses of people, watch television and there is actually a chance that some people who do not study it for a living will know or care what in blazes you are talking or writing about if you use TV as your oracle. Ideas about politics, culture, and the human condition, once considered the very raison d'être of criticism, might make some sort of a comeback. They might even once and for all crack the tough nut of mass culture . . . well, let's not get carried away. Suffice it to say that if TV is actually as evil as it is supposed to be, critical discoveries just might prove to be of some palpable value to society at large.

A victim of these adrenal thoughts, in 1975 I took time out from working on my master's thesis ("The Landscape of Language in William Wordsworth's *The Prelude*") to write a four-page essay about *The Mary Tyler Moore Show*, a sitcom that I liked despite several significant flaws (was I a budding critic or what?). I sent it to *The Village Voice*, which in those days had no TV section. It was accepted. I told all my friends and relatives about it. A week before scheduled publication it was killed by the editor. I certainly did not imagine at this point that I would go on to become a TV critic. In fact, had I known what a truly thankless, rotten, lousy job it was, I probably would have stuck with Coleridge, Wordsworth, Keats, and Shelley. I might at this very moment, as you are wondering whether to read, skim, or skip this page, chapter, or book, be heaving a pregnant sigh in front of a room of hopelessly indebted tuition-payers, fingering through yellowing notes on "Ode to a Nightingale," searching for something, anything, to divert youthful attention from the swells and surges of hormonal cueing mechanisms developed in the post-MTV environment. The truth is, however, far less beautiful.

There is no medium for the dissemination of drama, rhetoric, or any other art in which the opinions of commentators are less respected or cared about than television. Stageplays live and die by their notices. Readers of novels and other kinds of books, being readers, tend to read book reviews and continue in this way to practice what for the past two hundred years or so has, with self-gratifying effort, passed for high culture. Film criticism has become so popular that it appears not only in print, but on television itself: Two thumbs up! But TV viewers watch television and apparently don't seem to care very much to read about it or anything else (*TV Guide*'s status as the world's largest selling magazine notwithstanding). As if that is not problem enough, not a single program dedicated to television criticism appears on any of the national networks, including PBS, or on any of the scores of national cable services or, to my knowledge, on any of the hundreds of individual stations that hold FCC licenses "in the public interest."

AM talk-radio is apparently the sole mass communications venue for the public discussion of television in America. Unencumbered by the onus of the word "criticism," talk jocks have but to mention the name of one program that aired for three seasons in the mid-1970s and the switchboard is lit for the shift. But given the fact that the term "TV viewers" describes, roughly, the entire population of the United States, the audience for written TV comment is painfully miniscule. Who in fact does read the paltry scraps of TV criticism that do manage to appear in print? A pitifully marginal demographic hodgepodge, if you ask me.

People who claim not to have television sets, or at least not to watch them, make up a surprisingly large segment of the audience for books and articles about TV. This may seem paradoxical, but hostility toward television is a cheap signifier of breeding in America and the snobbish are always shopping for a new reason to make a point of why they do not care about things that are beneath them. These intellectual status trendoids are not drawn to any kind of a practical TV criticism that talks about what is actually on TV. Instead they dote on the related discipline of "media criticism," a thriving academic cottage industry dedicated to culturally messianic denunciations, mostly rote, but occasionally semi-innovative, concerning how and why television rots your brain cells or is causing the melt-down of Western civilization, secular humanism, Christianity, democratic socialism, or anything else that anyone can think of as worth holding dear in an age characterized by the adoration of quantity over the appreciation of quality.

The only other easily identifiable group that does not watch television profusely is the homeless, one of the fastest growing segments of the American population and, I might add, a group that seems to spend an inordinate amount of time at public libraries, though it's a pretty good guess that they haven't popped in to browse the media criticism shelves. You get the feeling that unlike the high-brows the homeless would be home watching TV if they could be, rather than out on bus stop benches sleeping under cover of big-ticket appliance boxes and the cast-off pages of yesterday's print media.

The consumer jackpot segment for TV criticism in this market economy is composed of college students. Unlike the homeless and the snobbish, this group watches plenty of TV and by now only certain tiny subsegments, such as ultra left-wing English majors, God knows what tendency, even bother to deny it. College students are moved to buy even the most expensive volumes of TV criticism by a profound conviction that any course with the word television in its title has got to be easier than Shakespeare, much less organic chemistry or calculus. As a result, they have made themselves the one-and-only captive audience for the small shelf-full of books of TV criticism that have been published. I know I speak for my colleagues when I express my appreciation to them for their patronage.

Is there potentially a wider audience for TV criticism than active snobs and passive college students? I ask this question with some urgency and as much sincerity as I can still muster. After writing three books and over one hundred articles for various magazines, newspapers, and journals on the subject, I have received exactly eleven pieces of mail from my loyal and not-so-loyal fans. In those letters I have been chided for characterizing Quentin McHale (Ernest Borgnine) as a noncommissioned officer on the sitcom *McHale's Navy,* when in fact he *was* a commissioned officer. I have been attacked by a resident of Quincy, Illinois, for taking an alliterative liberty with her home town when I dared suggest that Archie Bunker of *All in the Family* was a character more likely found there than in Queens, New York. I have been corrected as to exactly which season Michael Ontkean joined the cast of Aaron Spelling's copshow, *The Rookies.* I was even once—no kidding—lauded for my defense of British policy during the Falklands War, though I have never in my memory written a single word on the subject and to this day have not thought enough about it to hold anything like an opinion.

Literary critics have been no less eclectic than the public in their treatment of my work. Martha Bayles, a writer and editor for the *Wall Street Journal,* reviewed my second book, *Comic Visions* (a bargain at only $10.95), for the *Sunday New York Times Book Review.*[1] She was generally kind to the book, but admonished me for "wielding a Frankfurt School bludgeon" against TV, thus implying that she believed me to be a Marxist, no small charge considering the source. Lauren Rabinowitz, a professor of some important subject unknown to the Greeks, reviewed the same book for *American Quarterly,* an academic journal that with each new issue gives new meaning to the term "not-for-profit."[2] She was generally unkind to the book, accusing me of advocating a "reactionary program" in my approach to thinking about TV. In the shadowy, self-righteous chambers of academic political correctness (see segment 4), this is the moral equivalent of being charged with treason (though of course treason in the usual sense of the word is not generally looked upon as a crime by such thinkers). By focusing on the work of particular TV shows and their creator-producers, I was, to Professor Rabinowitz's kvetching dismay, promoting an insidious heritage of "masterpieces and geniuses." Having read her prose I grant her that she stands in little danger of ever getting mixed up with that unsavory crowd.

Like most American book writers, I cannot make a living writing and so I have had to hold a day job to support my inputting time at the keyboard. After brief career disorders in New York City as a taxi driver, a (pre-AIDS) venereal disease epidemiologist, and an NBC office boy, I moved from the West Side of Manhattan, my home after Binghamton, to Iowa City, Iowa, where I took a doctorate in a "discipline" known as "American studies" at the University of Iowa so as to make a credential that would allow me professoring jobs. This was much easier than I had imagined. Hardly anyone has the attention span, or what used to be called "the patience," to write or to write a lot anymore, and even fewer people are capable of giving that much discipline or energy to writing something that leads to a job that starts at about the same money as an assistant manager's position at a Seven-Eleven. So, if you write enough, no matter what you write, you can call it a dissertation and you will be awarded a doctorate just for showing the stamina. This does not mean that all dissertations are bad, just that bad ones are good enough to get you a membership card in the professor's union if they tip the postal scales at about a pound or so and the majority of the sentences have subjects and agreeing predicates (well maybe just subjects and predicates).

The advantages of university life in America are obvious. The three greatest, as even the greenest of graduate students will tell you, are June, July, and August. But if you want to dance through long summer vacations in the Mediterranean breeze, dear careerists, you've got to pay the piper. It is my sad duty to report that the faculties of our major universities are dominated by a squadron of bureaucratic personalities so petty in their insistences, so narrowly focused in their concerns, so utterly nervous about the wild discrepancies they perceive dividing their capacities from their pay checks, as to make any given faculty meeting on any given day at any given institution of higher learning appear to be a kind of collective hysterical nervous breakdown.

Here is a group of people who take it as an article of faith that the world would be a better place if only they were allowed to run it and yet, at the same time, will not hesitate to acrimony, the double-cross, or even blackmail over office supply budgets. Life among such is the special cross borne by virtually all American intellectuals as well as by writers and artists of many stripes who are forced to search for affordable health insurance in the eerie education factories run by this stunning collection of high-I.Q. hicks, hacks, nerds, dweebs, blockheads, boors, and ultrasensitive nincompoops. Worse than ancient Athens? Probably. Better than the Gulag? Well, I guess. Worse or better than working at a television network, movie studio, recording company, or cable outfit? The answer to this last question contains more than a few clues to the fate of American culture.

After picking up my terminal sheepskin and mailing it to my mother back in Brooklyn for safekeeping (none of the half dozen universities that have since employed me—nor anyone else besides my mother—has ever actually asked to see it), I left Iowa City to begin a career that sent me in ritual fulfillment of my ethnic destiny wandering around in search of teaching jobs to support my writing habit. My own private diaspora took me first to New England, that bedrock slab of American culture, spending three years in sleazy Providence, Rhode Island, a city that looks to 1920s Chicago rather than the U.S. Constitution for its model of government. But at least while there I had the good fortune to be working at Brown, a well-run school with friendly and serious students and colleagues, located in the only part of town that fails to qualify as an urban nightmare.

Then my luck ran out. I made the near fatal mistake of accepting a job at Brandeis University, a broke and broken institution whose faculty had been reduced to a pack of rats clawing at an ever-diminishing piece of cheese. Brandeis was by far the most depressing place in which I'd ever spent more than a few minutes. The students were paying Harvard prices for a state college product and didn't know whether to be emotionally distraught or to make believe it wasn't really happening and that college was as much fun as it was supposed to be. The faculty was composed of two primary elements: tenured fossils, who repeated mantra-like anecdotes about what a great place the school had been in the 1960s; and the junior faculty, mostly resentful spouses of people who had good jobs in the area and were thus condemned to struggle for tenure at a school whose intellectual life was dominated by the issue of whether graduate students from Taiwan should be allowed to eat *trafe* on campus. As if this nurturing environment was not blessing enough, doing four years at Brandeis also meant doing a stretch in and around Boston, an insufferably snot-nosed city whose visions of grandeur, never in short supply, are based on its position as the Detroit of America's higher education assembly lines.

In 1989 I quit a tenure-track job, voluntarily giving up health, dental, and retirement benefits, mostly out of disgust with Brandeis, but at least partially out of an attempt to retain some kind of epic vision of the self or at least a bit of self-respect. Never quite able to dig the surrealist possibilities of living in a Kafka-like terror of Kafka scholars, I have been paying my cable bills ever since with a variety of free-lance writing and year-to-year temporary teaching jobs, living in Los Angeles, a place where people are amazed to learn that you've read a book, much less written one. This is not as bad as it sounds. If the book has no pictures in it, the natives can become downright reverent and will even invite you to parties to improve their social status, which, just as all the media stereotypes indicate, is the definitive activity and goal of all life in this part of the world. No one in Los Angeles will be offended by this picture of the city as long as I don't forget to mention that the weather is good. Indeed, it is. Seventy-eight degrees and sunny just about every day. And the cable? More channels than a NASA ground station during the grave-yard shift.

I have become a traveling salesman of ideas. I drive around the freeways of Southern California from classroom to classroom, from li-brary to gym, from parking structure to parking structure, cursing at the traffic, grimacing at the smog, listening to the radio, and thinking about what to say to the confused and confusing future leaders of America: the Santa Monica Freeway east to USC for "Aesthetics of Television," the Pasadena Freeway north to Cal Tech for "Introduction to the Essay," the San Diego Freeway south to La Jolla for "History and Criticism of American Broadcasting," a short spin out Sunset Boulevard for "TV and Society" at UCLA. I'm ready for my check, Mr. Diploma Mill. I *am* big; the ideas got small. T. W. Adorno, eat your heart out.

Oh yes, and there are several other autobiographical details I might mention. In addition to being a chronically dissatisfied, loudmouthed déclassé Polish-Romanian Jew from New York City, I'm also an angry and testy homosexual who is watching his TV these days from a futon couch in an overpriced apartment in the heart of the West Hollywood gay ghetto. I'm an enthusiastic supporter of the legalization of marijuana, especially if it will help bring prices down. I've suffered several clinical depressive episodes, including one that followed the murder, in a street crime in New Orleans, of my domestic partner of ten years.

In a better world, these last several items might not be as important as the quality of what is said in this book about its subject: the evolving role of literacy in a multimedia communications environment. The men-tioning of such personal details might even be considered gratuitous. But apparently, to the few hearty souls who still read, this kind of demo-graphic profile seems to have become critically important. Faith in meta-phor, logic, and language has been waning through most of my lifetime. There is a feeling that these old apparatuses of consciousness, once used to pry apart and reconnect minds and souls and comrades and debates, can now be regarded as no more than weapons of manipulation. As a result people want to know beforehand whether to be for or against—whether to hate or to love, advocate or oppose, cherish or fear—what they are about to read, based on the credentials of the author: race, gender, lust affinity, political belief, personal injury inventory, and so on.

I hate it that this is the awful cul-de-sac at which writing and the life-of-the-mind in general have become stalled. But I'm still determined to be a writer and there is no writing without readers. So I must tell you I am approximately as proud and ashamed of myself and all the things that I've done and said as anyone and I don't give a shit who knows it, even though I don't have tenure or even any kind of a real full-time job anymore and I pay my own health insurance and it's pretty goddamned expensive.

If Americans are, as Emerson cracked in his 1837 address to the Harvard Phi Beta Kappa Society, "a people too busy" for artistic or aesthetic concerns, why do so many of us spend so much time watching television?[3] The easy answer is that TV has nothing to do with the arts, and our watching it merely proves the enduring truth of Emerson's point. In effect we are an audience for commercial television *instead* of for the arts, or, as Calvin Coolidge put it, "the business of America is business." There is plenty of evidence to support this thesis. Much of it is summarized in this powerful one-liner reported by broadcasting historian William Boddy: "When television producer William Froug was hired as a Hollywood executive in charge of drama . . . a CBS executive instructed him, 'Your job is to produce shit.' "[4]

A more troubling answer is that television has made us so thoroughly interested in drama, current events, spectator sports, illustrated music, monology, travelogues, the weather, old movies, new movies, gastronomy, animated cartoons, shopping, politically didactic religious sermons, sexual voyeurism, gossip, home improvement techniques, and *Jeopardy* that we are too busy for almost anything else, such as, let's say, reading. As succinctly put by Dr. Frank Stanton, a man whose relationship to American cultural history is something like that of a faith healer's to medicine, "the public interest is what the public is interested in."[5]

People, or what Communists used to call The People, or what social scientists call the pool from which the sample is drawn, watch a lot of television. Do they like it? Do they need it? Both? Does TV aid in the intellectual stimulation of the population by exposing people to information and ideas that they would not likely encounter otherwise? Does TV preclude the intellectual stimulation of the population by diverting people from information and ideas with attractively packaged infantile fantasies? Both? Is TV-watching a self-destructive activity? For most people? For you? For others? Both? If you weren't watching TV, what would you be doing? Would you rather be watching TV than reading this book?

Television has changed the way that people get to know things, making schools, books, historical continuity, and other basic learning structures and tools feel antiquarian, archaic, or perhaps even obsolete. This is particularly frightening to anyone who still uses the literate way of knowing and who values the results. The contradictions between a career as a writer and a life as an American constantly send me scurrying back and forth across charged fields dividing rational, case-building, thought-made expression from the effortless satisfactions of image scan: a temple of the mind and a marketplace of the body.

1. Martha Bayles, "Taking Sitcoms Seriously," *New York Times Sunday Book Review* 30 April 1989, 30.

2. Lauren Rabinovitz, "Television Criticism and American Studies," *American Quarterly* 43, no. 2 (June 1991): 358–70.

3. Ralph Waldo Emerson, "The American Scholar," *The Portable Emerson,* ed. Mark Van Doren (New York: Viking, 1946), 23.

4. William Boddy, *Fifties Television* (New York: Oxford Univ. Press, 1993), 238.

5. Ibid., 239.

"... but a semblance of randomness always returns."

Literacy
Love It or Leave It

Read 'em and Weep

In Japan, a consumer pays approximately eight times the world price for a kilo of rice, despite the fact that rice is a primary staple of the national diet. How does this occur in a nation whose thrift is otherwise legendary in the modern world? The Japanese government has deemed—or at least conceded the point—that the production of rice from Japanese soil is a metaphysical necessity the significance of which outweighs the normally pragmatic considerations of a market economy. Theoretically, the nutritional needs of the Japanese people might be met just as well by less expensive rice imported from Texas. But for spiritual reasons, for reasons based in national religious and philosophic traditions, the otherwise inefficient cultivation of rice on Japan's "postage-stamp size" farms continues, preserved by strong, active state intervention.

Many or most Japanese people apparently support this policy as demonstrated by their willingness to shoulder, without protest, the economic burden it creates. Most economic theories indicate, however, that if the state removed its protectionist tariffs, thus allowing for the sale of imported rice at one-eighth of current levels, some consumers would take advantage of the bargain and, gradually—considering Japanese reverence for tradition, it might take generations—the market share of domestically grown rice would shrink or perhaps even become marginal. One can imagine an eventual situation in which domestic rice has gained a kind of ritualistic function in Japanese culture, used on holidays and special religious occasions, much as kosher wines are used in North America by many Jewish families who do not otherwise observe religious dietary laws or normally care for syrupy sweet reds.

25

American literacy, like the sacred rice of Japan, has become increasingly dependent on a spiritually motivated, interventionist policy for its strength in the domestic communications market. We are faced with the spectacle of people growing up in a culture where they are blanketed with electronic audiovisual messages from the moment they are born, learning most of what they know about social relations, current events, the national heritage, and what society expects of them from nonprint media, notably television, film, radio, and recorded music. Though children are taught to read in the school system beginning in the early grades, the role of literacy in their lives outside of the classroom becomes increasingly remote.

The decline of public education in the United States is pretty much taken for granted these days, the subject of much hand-wringing and exasperation. The public schools have become a convenient scapegoat for our inability as a society to cope with the discrepancy between a collective reverence for literacy and the realpolitik of how information is now collected and distributed to people. The religious right blames the godless classroom of the public school for Johnny's reading problem, hoping to circumvent the Constitution and receive public monies and tax credits by declaring itself the savior of literacy. The I-don't-wanna-pay-taxes crowd votes to cut public school budgets, then points to the decline of literacy and advocates further budget cuts to prevent throwing good money after bad. The private college advocates, through their professional associations and alumni groups, lobby against money for state universities as they jack up their astronomical tuition fees and make lifetime guaranteed loan slaves out of students who should have gone to public colleges.

But if the horse is to be put before the cart, it is the decline of reading and writing, not the decline of the public schools, that should really be the primary focus of discussion. If educated people were, generally speaking, better at these skills a hundred years ago than they are today, it is probably because they had more practice at them. The telephone, for example, turned letter writing from an organic necessity of middle-class life into an antiquarian art form, much as the camera turned painting from a practical documentary technique into an aesthetic ordeal. During this same period, broadcasting and film subsumed the routine storytelling functions of the culture, both journalistic and fictional, mostly at the expense of print forms such as newspapers and books. Even pornographic literature suffered as the VCR offered masturbators and other consumers the advantages of videotape. Much of the reading material that survives becomes progressively dependent on illustration and graphic design to keep an audience; *USA Today,* with its tiny blocks of print set among large splashes of color, shape, and narrative image might hardly be recognizable as a newspaper to a nineteenth-century reader. Go down to the mall and check out the calendars, datebooks, books-on-tape, photography albums, graphic novels (once known as comic books), computer software packages, and videotapes that have conquered the shelf space once held by the alphabet-dominated units at the "bookstore." Have these contractions of reading and writing been matched by any noteworthy areas of literary expansion? Did I miss one somewhere? Well, there is the proliferation of computer manuals.

By the time we get to video games thought processes are reoriented away from the interpretation of abstract symbols, which is essential to literate activity, and toward direct stimulus-response through eye-hand coordination. There is an undeniable pleasure, an enjoyment with primitive credentials, in cutting out the intense cognitive operations that are necessary to read and to instead "just do"—with joystick or keypad— whatever must be done in order to solve the immediate, if essentially idiotic, problems posed by a video game.

Reading a book opens a conduit from page to eye to body. The ink alphabet signs are transformed into meanings and images that penetrate the body as irony, fear, anger, and so on, stimulating the emotional capacities for empathy and sympathy. The body is seduced and entertained as the mind is instructed. Consider these two passages from Don DeLillo's *White Noise* (each taken from a different part of the novel):

> You have to learn how to look. You have to open yourself to the data. TV offers incredible amounts of psychic data. It opens ancient memories of world birth, it welcomes us into the grid, the network of little buzzing dots that make up the picture pattern. There is light, there is sound. . . . What more do you want? Look at the wealth of data concealed in the grid, in the bright packaging, the jingles, the slice-of-life commercials, the products hurtling out of darkness, the coded messages and endless repetitions, like chants, like mantras. '*Coke is it, Coke is it, Coke is it*'. The medium practically overflows with sacred formulas if we can remember how to respond innocently and get past our irritation, weariness and disgust.[1]

And,

> the supermarket shelves have been rearranged. It happened one day without warning. There is agitation and panic in the aisles, dismay in the faces of older shoppers. They walk in a fragmented trance, stop and

go, clusters of well-dressed figures frozen in the aisles, trying to figure out the pattern, discern the underlying logic, trying to remember where they'd seen the Cream of Wheat. They see no reason for it, find no sense in it. The scouring pads are with the hand soap now, the condiments are scattered. The older the man or woman, the more carefully dressed and groomed. Men in Sansabelt slacks and bright knit shirts. Women with a powdered and fussy look, a self-conscious air, prepared for some anxious event. They turn into the wrong aisle, peer along the shelves, sometimes stop abruptly, causing other carts to run into them. Only the generic food is where it was, white packages plainly labeled. The men consult lists, the women do not.[2]

Each of these passages is a meditation on a familiar and seemingly mundane constituent of contemporary American life: TV (consumer communication) and supermarket (consumption climax). They are complementary echoes of a realized personality, witty and discerning, each generously offering transformation and transcendence to the reader. Intellectual sensations become indistinguishable from visceral reactions as the concentrated allusional resonances of words, phrases, and verbal gestures burst into a needle-shower of associations: a kind of shiatsu massage of the brain, sending pinpricks of cerebral sensation flowing out across the neural system. Achieving a state of seamlessness between mind and body is among the paramount pleasures that reading can offer. (Speaking personally, it is my favorite.) But of course only a few books or authors ever afford readers such experiences and the activity of reading, per se, should not be confused with the exceptional experiences of the best that reading has to offer.

Playing a video game also creates a conduit of information flow: from screen to eye to body. With the video game, however, it is not the capacity for imaginative identification that is stimulated, but rather the capacity to act quickly and decisively. I play Alexey Pazhitnov's *Tetris* almost every day, sometimes for as much as an hour.[3] The seven shapes come tumbling down from the top of the screen. The middle three fingers of my right hand manipulate them with the keypad buttons, pushing them right and left, turning them upside down, fitting them into the empty spaces. Correct decisions produce faint waves of satisfaction. Incorrect decisions generate similar modulations of frustration. Occasionally a suspicion arises that the computer program is creating difficult or impossible situations, but a semblance of randomness always returns. If I break into my top ten high scores, I am filled with a moment of competence. If I fail to break into my top ten scores, I play again or put it away and struggle with some other activity or I watch television. If I play too much or too little I have *Tetris* dreams in which I triumph over extremely difficult dilemmas or suffer the consequences.

Consider how cheaply imaginative identification can be had from TV and other household gadgets these days, then add to that the problem of living in a highly organized corporate society where quick decisive actions are generally suspect. It is quite possible to conclude that the video game is offering today's player more of what is missing from life, which is an essential function of art. Given the fact that you are reading this, there is more than a chance that you are offended, disturbed, or flabbergasted that I am suggesting that the programming of video games has become an art form on an equal footing with the writing of books, let alone a more essential one. After all, look at the two DeLillo passages: writing that meets the challenges of contemporary experience with grace, passion, insight, and humor. But although it is easy to demonstrate the virtues of the novel by offering DeLillo's prose in support of my own, can I possibly do similar justice to *Tetris*? How can I describe the quality of my appreciation of it or the function that this (stupid?) game fulfills in my life? Is addiction a more appropriate word than appreciation? There are times when I just can't stop playing—more times than when I just can't stop reading. Are ardent readers "addicted" to reading? If you were scanning a CD-ROM instead of reading this in a book I might be in a better position to make a case for the pleasures of *Tetris*.

Literacy is basically a practice. There is no substitute for personal daily organic involvement with reading and writing if you want to master the process. The less time you spend at it, the less skill you are bound to acquire or hold. As people make greater use of nonliterate, semiliterate, and aliterate media for the day-to-day conducting of their business and leisure, and thus for the day-to-day construction of their consciousnesses, the getting of an educational credential remains one of the few tangible incentives to read and write. What was the means to many ends during the halcyon days of rising massive literacy (a period running roughly between the mid-eighteenth and mid-twentieth centuries) becomes, too often now, an end unto itself. This is a particularly unhappy development for anyone harboring a political belief that the evangelization of literacy is, by itself, a fundamental step toward the social improvement of humanity.

Among the managerial classes of American society (or what once might have been thought of as the "reading classes"), the university performs an interventionist function on behalf of literacy, inflating its value by tying it to the receipt of a diploma, which functions as a kind of union card for middle-class status, though not necessarily middle-class life in consumer society. The remoteness of literacy, hardly mitigated by the general chaos of high school or by the standardized multiple-choice examinations that get a person admitted to college, suddenly disintegrates as the need for literacy skills slams right into the face of an entering freshman. All of a sudden finding the time, space, and attention-span for reading thousands of pages in a matter of weeks and for writing frequent short essays and long, detailed reports becomes a priority problem—in many cases for the first and only time in the life of an American. Many cope with the situation and, at least under the conditions of being college students, become competently literate. Among those who do not, some drop out and others find a way around the reading-and-writing dilemma and graduate anyway.

This last group of innovators is worth considering. Yes, even at college, that supposed last bastion and obstacle course of literacy, there are various ways to get by without having to spend outrageous blocks of time sitting still in front of books. Some students minimize the burden of print by seeking out courses with professors who will award grades based on feelings. In this method, the quantitative demands of reading can be alleviated by using only a chapter or perhaps even a few passages from an assigned book as a springboard for a self-therapeutic monologue.[4] This allows the student to concentrate on the *writing* of the paper, which is trouble enough, without having to waste all that time on the reading. The most extreme example of this that I ever saw was the case of a forty-five-page senior honors thesis in American Studies at Brandeis University. The project was supposedly about one entire novel, *The Virginian* by Owen Wister. But it only made reference to three different pages in the book, each of which was cited in the footnotes over and over again. (Aristotle might be happy to know that these three key pages were symmetrically spaced, as if to represent beginning, middle, and end.)

The upshot of the thesis was that the writer was convinced that the male narrator of the novel was in love with the Virginian but that he was too closeted to admit it. This made the thesis writer, who was gay, feel hurt, angry, rebellious, and resentful of the homophobic traditions of American society. He took the opportunity to describe those feelings in some detail. I told him I could not recommend the paper for departmental honors at graduation because of the minimum of research that had gone into this research project. Did he see similar homosexual overtones in other Wister novels or nonfiction writings? Was there any historical evidence concerning Wister's sexual orientation? What might the consequences have been of a public profession of homosexual love by the narrator of an American novel and specifically of a Western novel around the turn of the century? Had any critics—any critic at all—ever commented on the subject of this thesis? His response was to accuse me of betraying him. After all he had picked me for his advisor because I was "out." He had imagined me a member of an old fag network that he could join, but instead I had just turned out to be an old fag.

Another way to enhance the appearance of literate activity—and to beef up the prestigious footnote section without spending a lot of time staring at ink—is to use just one book, preferably an anthology, and cite all the quotations used in the paper as if they had been taken from the original sources. I received a definitive example of such a paper while teaching a graduate seminar called "Interpreting Popular Culture" at the University of Southern California. There were three law students in the class that semester who had chosen the course as their one non-law school elective. This choice was based on the stated premise that they were going into entertainment law and the unstated premise that in the academic world the phrase "popular culture" really means "basket weaving." During that semester two of the three engaged in activities that can be generously described as ethically questionable—probably a respectable showing for lawyers (bah-boom).

One of the budding legal eagles handed in a final paper that included four and a half pages of footnotes, jacking up the page total by about 25 percent. All of them came from a single text, an anthology of essays titled *Mass Culture: The Popular Arts in America.*[5] That book, however, was never cited anywhere by the writer. Instead each article used in the paper was cited to the original point of publication, as if the student had read, or at least leafed through, a pile of books instead of just one. To add a bit of overkill, the secondary quotations that occurred within these articles were cited as if those were read (or at least physically handled) as well. Because I had actually read the *Mass Culture* book, I caught on right away, which made me feel like quite the accomplished scholar (now if I could only read Latin). I gave the paper—permissive me—a "C" and told the student the reason why. Without fully understanding my clinical critique of his documentation practices, he denied whatever it was that I had accused him of and threatened to sue me for something that I, in turn, wasn't quite able to understand. I have yet to be served with papers.

Another officer-of-the-court-in-training in that particular class handed in an essay that had nothing whatever to do with the assignment I had given; it was probably written for another course. As it was the first paper of the semester—once again, permissive me—I decided to give the student a chance to start fresh and hand in another paper. She responded by calling me a "dickhead" and dropping the course.

To be fair, students aren't the only ones looking for ways around the reading problem. Faculty, despite all attempts to hide it, are Americans living in TV land, too. Trying to explain "the disappearance of reading," in his book *The Pleasures of Reading in an Ideological Age*, Robert Alter laments the unabashed lack of enthusiasm that so many literature professors nowadays profess for literature. Some post-mod lit profs even propose the abolition of literature departments, hoping to replace them with "discourse" departments in which "instructors would be free to teach Shakespeare, television scripts, government memoranda, comic books, and advertising copy in a single program as instances of the language of power."[6] Personally, I would advocate the teaching of all of these print genres by anyone who has anything worthwhile to say about them. But the descending quantity of pages on Alter's list of avant-garde literary genres is salient. Even people who read for a living are at loose ends to find ways to cope with the demands that reading make, which are so extraordinary to the requirements and rhythms of life as it is now lived in the G-7 countries. You practically need a grant to read *Middlemarch*.

The search for a quiet place and an uninterrupted time quite frankly makes reading a pain in the neck and a pain in the neck is something that might be tolerated for good reason (e.g., the getting of a diploma or tenure), but it is not something that is loved. Who loves reading? (This is so sad.) Who can teach reading appreciation with a pure heart and a straight face? Who can soliloquize on the rhapsodic stimulation of listening to the silent voice of ink? I tell you the corps is dwindling. Television offers voice, sight, sound, and personality prepacked, intact. With books, the availability of these things depends on the reader's willingness to collaborate with the writer. Reading demands work and shuts you out unless you put your nose to the grindstone. TV invites you to exercise your right to relax. There is a tendency that has survived the trials of evolution to seek the path of least resistance.

Alter relates the story of a student who read *Moby Dick*, a big fat book by a dead white male about a big fat white sea mammal. She liked it despite the fact that she had been warned off it by two English professors who informed her that it was "a bore and scarcely worth the effort of reading." Freely granting that *Moby Dick* is not the greatest novel ever written, Alter contends that "a teacher of literature who dismisses it as too much of a bore to read might be better off teaching computer science or selling insurance."[7] Or perhaps such a teacher would be better off offering a seminar on "Ten Great Government Memoranda" or "The Baroque Magazine Ad." But in any case a literature teacher with neither the attention span to read Melville, nor a sense of shame about not having the attention span to read Melville, although an honest citizen, is not likely to do formidable battle against the forces in contemporary life that have lined up against literacy.

Imagine, *hypocrite lecteur,* that you are required to learn some information for your job over the course of several days. You are offered the choice of a book or a videotape as a source. Which would you choose? The book might be short—let's say a hundred pages. But how long does a hundred pages take to read? Two hours? Two days? Two weeks? It really depends on the hundred pages. Try a hundred pages of T. S. Eliot's "Notes Toward the Definition of Culture" if you don't believe me. The videotape could be a long one—let's say four hours. But at least it would be *just* four hours, a finite amount of time, something that can be dealt with and provided for in a world defined by schedules and appointments. Even if it is as difficult a visual text as, say, Luis Buñuel's *The Milky Way,* you could still run it through the VCR, stay in the room, and believe you've "seen" it. While watching the videotape it would be possible to eat, drink, smoke, take notes with both hands, and get up and walk around without "losing" any time. Is it any wonder that some people are only able to discover the joys of literacy in prison?[8]

But not all the advantages are with the videotape. If, for example, you had to offer a written analysis of what you had learned to your boss, you might give the book a chance. Research—the finding and reviewing of explicit details—is an activity that for the moment remains better suited to print than videotape. Despite increasingly sophisticated scanning mechanisms, specific bits of information are just too difficult to access from a videotape. The optimal situation of course would be to have both video and book at hand. This idea, as simple as it sounds, can be disturbing to the conservative literary sensibility that will concede no more than the status of "audiovisual aid" to nonprint media.

It is much more than an afterthought to this discussion to point out that the value of either item, book, or videotape (or for that matter any humanly produced expression) is ultimately dependent upon the clarity and quality of meaning that the creator of the work has given it. Anyone who argues that a poorly written book is an inherently superior source of information to a well-made videotape is focusing on the issue of his or her personal status rather than on the issue of communication.

The simultaneous persistence of reverence for, and the decline of love for, reading is perhaps most tragically manifest in the almost universal indifference toward bad writing. "In some circles," Alter observes, "it is now regarded as an intellectual virtue to write badly or obscurely, with at least one prominent literary scholar having raised the banner of 'difficulty' as the very aim and emblem of critical prose."[9] This is particularly daunting for literate culture in America because academics are the ones who have been charged with the duty of teaching people how to write. Has a student with Melville's writing talent or a tenth of Melville's writing talent ever taken a course with one of those professors who finds Melville too boring to read? What rotten luck for the probook forces.

Faced with entire classes of students, even graduate students, who cannot write competently, many professors go into a state of deep denial in response to the absurd situation in which they find themselves. Some choose to disregard writing, as if it is a separate subject, and grade students on the "content" of their papers, as if that can somehow be considered apart from the medium in which it is being expressed. Professors, even English professors, often complain that they were not hired to teach grammar and so disregard the particulars of student errors, perhaps taking off a half a grade at the end of the essay for "poorly written" if the thing is downright incomprehensible. Students who are chastised for the likes of grammatical errors or incoherence (style is an "advanced" problem that almost never comes up anymore) protest that they didn't sign up for a composition course. The result is that both teachers and students hate "the writing problem" and wish it away to a "writing program," as if, like nuclear physics, it could be a subject for specialists teaching special courses.

The lack of care about good writing runs deep in American academic thinking. Perhaps the trial of reading bad student writing rekindles Puritan, Catholic, or Judaic faith in the redemptive nature of pain. I was actually chewed out by the chair of the American Studies Department at Brandeis for "hounding" students about their writing ("This is not an English Department!"). That same chairman also admonished me for publishing articles in the *Village Voice* and *The Atlantic* because these "nonrefereed journals" (actual words used by chairman) stressed "general readability over scholarly precision" and, perhaps even more damning, they don't include any footnotes. I responded by asking him, in a letter, if he thought that the articles I had written were any good. He refused to answer. I resigned. (In all fairness I should mention that this guy absolutely hated my guts and wanted me out of the place because I was gay and he may not even have meant any of the things he said that were critical of my work. He once advised an Orthodox Jewish student to not choose me for a thesis advisor because my interests were "more Hellenic than Hebraic." I only found out about this because the student asked me what that meant. I did my best to explain; he fled from my office in terror.)

These not-all-that-unusual examples notwithstanding, the demands of the diploma quest may well bring about temporary improvement in the reading and writing capabilities of people who spend several years doing coursework at universities; practice can bring results for those who choose to take advantage of the opportunity. But unfortunately, the university's severe intervention on behalf of literacy ends as abruptly as it begins, leaving reading and writing skills to go stale in a society that doesn't seem to have much organic use for them. And so the credibility gap widens between the stated aims of American education and the demonstrated needs of American society. This makes the schools—and the people who have taught in them and attended them—look awfully foolish.

It's Only Words

Given the embedded traditions of logocentricity in Western consciousness, it is not surprising that a reverence for literacy is outlasting a love for it. Evidence of belief in the transcendental power of the word pervades language and culture. As the Bible tells it, the universe itself came into being by means of the word ("Let there be light"). A man and a woman risk mortal sin in sexual union, unless they are "pronounced" husband and wife. The state will void its own most basic principle and take the life of a citizen who is "sentenced" to death. Every time a magician says "abra-cadabra" before pulling a rabbit out of a hat, ritual homage is paid to the mystical authority of the word to change reality.

The advent of moveable type in the sixteenth century greatly enhanced the already powerful position of the word. The printing press extended language beyond oral and temporal limits by allowing for its mechanical reproduction on documents, and thus its mass diffusion. The spoken word, after all, was a visceral medium, an instrument of human dimensions. It was eclipsed by the written word, a transmission system that drove communication in a single direction, oblivious to immediate corporal response. The very existence of a published text—the industrial "miracle" of the book—was evidence of the power and wisdom that stood behind it. Nothing that anyone could tell you had as much authority as that which had been set in type. At least once every several months this point is reiterated to me at close range as I stand in the supermarket check-out line and listen to people argue over the veracity of tabloid stories about three-headed babies, alien abductions or miracle diet pills that take off weight while you sleep: "Do you think they could print it if it wasn't true?" If I did not know that my neighbors were so heavily armed I might reply, "Yeah, and who do you think is gonna stop them?"

Another consequence of the rise of print culture was to put the oral-based culture of the family on the defensive; it has yet to recover. Experts (i.e., writers of books) put in ink everything from recipes to medical remedies to prescriptions for temporal success and eternal salvation. The book on the shelf in the home was a message from a greater outside source. It was a harbinger of the coming to the home of the radio, the television, the on-line computer data-base, and other components of a vast and vertical electronic culture system that would have the effect of trivializing kinship relationships and atomizing the members of the household. Who is to be believed when Grandma comes into conflict with Julia Child?

Religion, art, and politics were all transformed by the mechanically reproduced word during the age of the printing press. The ritual chant of the Catholic mass was challenged by the book-wielding Protestant ministry. The reformed churches of the print world promoted a spiritual faith buttressed by direct quotation of chapter and verse; the faithful were even taught to read. The mystical transformations of the Eucharist were made subordinate to a lecture on the "main idea" of a story. Transcriptions of sermons even survive on college literature syllabi today, much to the *auteur* glory of Cotton Mather and Jonathan Edwards, if not necessarily God.

Western literature, which had been dominated since antiquity by primary oral forms—notably stage drama and poetry—shifted its focus during the eighteenth and nineteenth century to the novel, a variety of narrative designed specifically to be experienced in solitude by a silent individual decoding abstract symbols from the face of a printed page. In politics, the printing press allowed for the mass-produced pamphlet, a new print genre designed to be read by new reading classes. This literature included such revolutionary works as Thomas Paine's *Common Sense*, the Declaration of Independence, and Friedrich Engels' and Karl Marx's *Communist Manifesto*.

As the feudal order was overturned in Western countries, emerging middle-class societies invested their claims of legitimacy in a print culture of charters and declarations, a materialist culture that dismissed or downgraded unwritten traditions (the divine right of kings, or the privileges of birth) as mystical and irrational. European book writers including Charles Darwin, Sigmund Freud, and Emile Zola expressed and shaped the *imago mundi* of bourgeois society by offering rationalist explanations of the eternal mysteries—creation, romance, human cruelty—to readers whose faith in their own merit supported their rational claims to the right of governance. Universities shed their once primary religious affiliations to become centers of secular humanism—and that meant centers of book cultivation.

The chapel yielded to the library—the great warehouse of books—as the center of scholastic spirit and mission. Among the modern priest-class of professors and technocrats, bibliography replaced personal revelation as the currency of wisdom. The book became the flag of reason-based, middle-class humanistic idealism. Publishing books, not saving souls, could get a scholar tenure, which had to serve as a quick substitute for a heaven that was increasingly unavailable. And then of course there arose a cult that believed publishing books to be, all by itself, a soul-saving activity.

Perhaps the confusion of symbol and substance was inevitable; in any case, by the twentieth century, the book stood as the absolute and unchallenged focal point of the humanities, even at the expense of the broader concerns of language and art. Value and status were awarded to nonliterary arts and artists by the degree of literary response they stimulated. Oil painting and symphonic music did well in this regard while cartooning and boogie-woogie music did not.

The media hegemony of the book in high culture stands in stark contrast to the media fluidity of popular culture, where new tools for human expression and perception win resounding acceptance virtually as soon as they jump out of the lab—dime-novel, silent cinema, sound cinema, radio broadcast, telecast, cable, VCR—all bumping each other from the spotlight within the course of a century. Even in the area of media criticism, television programs such as *Siskel and Ebert* and *Entertainment Tonight* supersede in reach and influence any books that have been written on the subject of popular culture. In popular culture the written word is considered slow and user-unfriendly and is avoided or abbreviated wherever possible (whatever gets u thru the nite).

Literature is a communication system and literary criticism or, more broadly, humanistic belles lettres is an attempt to evaluate the system's sense and effectiveness. But this kind of critical writing has only been of marginal importance in the evaluation of the cultural communications systems that have surrounded, bypassed, and remade the role of literature in society in the last hundred years. T. W. Adorno was one of the many critics who helped to trivialize the humanities in the age of mass media. In 1954 he wrote,

> the effect of television cannot be adequately expressed in terms of success or failure, likes or dislikes, approval or disapproval. Rather an attempt should be made, with the aid of depth-psychological categories

and previous knowledge of mass media, to crystallize a number of theoretical concepts by which the potential effect of television—its impact upon various layers of the spectator's personality—could be studied.[10]

Call the guys in the lab coats; personal response is of no use here. While the humanities critics of the older systems (a.k.a. the "fine" arts) continue to study the work and its effects upon their own consciousnesses, the social science critics of the newer systems (especially television) choose to study the work's effects upon its receivers (i.e., the audience). A story told in print is greeted or rejected as an aesthetic event, while a story told on a TV screen reaches the world of learning as a sociological event. This petty little turf deal goes a long way in explaining the educational system's incompetence in dealing with the mass media or with a population that has been "unduly" shaped by it.

By ignoring and stereotyping the vital new vessels of language and imagination, the humanities have placed themselves at the margins of contemporary thinking. Valued more by the university as an antiquarian ornament than a dynamic epistemology—sort of like a charmingly nostalgic if somewhat dysfunctional old building that the campus just wouldn't be the same without—the humanities take the brunt of budget cuts, command the lowest salaries for teachers, and generally survive as poor relations to the sciences, the social sciences, and the physical education department.

As pure print mutates into a progressively picturesque form of communication in the so-called real world, students, or "education consumers" as they are now more accurately called, identify their interests and career requirements elsewhere. At some schools a college graduate's only contact with an English department may well be the taking of a "service course," the sole purpose of which is to teach academic protocol (i.e., literacy) for the writing of papers for other courses.[11] Similarly, the traditional foreign language requirement may now be satisfied in some programs with the study of a computer language.[12]

That humanities professors (and lovers of books, art, culture, and the rest of that stuff) are alarmed is understandable. The prevailing strategy of response, however, has only exacerbated the problem. Like panicking workers whose jobs are threatened by automation, many are calling for protectionist political intervention. Allan Bloom's *The Closing of the American Mind* (1987) remains a rallying cry for this position. Bemoaning the fact that even the highly educated—even his own blood relatives with graduate degrees—no longer read, he writes,

When they talk about heaven and earth, the relations between men and women, parents and children, the human condition, I hear nothing but cliches, superficialities, the material of satire. I am not saying anything so trite as that a life based on the Book is closer to the truth, that it provides the material for deeper research in and access to the real nature of things. Without the great revelations, epics and philosophies as part of our natural vision, there is nothing to see out there, and eventually little left inside. The Bible is not the only means to furnish a mind, but without a book of similar gravity, read with the gravity of the potential believer, it will remain unfurnished.[13]

"Our students," concludes Bloom, "have lost the practice of and the taste for reading. They have not learned how to read, nor do they have the expectation of delight or improvement from reading."[14] This is certainly true. But if this is a problem, what is a solution? A metaphysically based appeal to the dean's office—or to the federal government—to intervene on behalf of The Book by implementing required "Great Books" reading lists? The redneck humanists who have survived the late Professor Bloom seem to think so.

Even if teachers and students were forced by armed soldiers under the command of President William Bennett to read, discuss, and write about books by Plato, Matthew Arnold, and Allan Bloom, what would be the likely result? The humanities, a structure of epistemology based on the imaginative capacity for personal discovery through sympathy, empathy, humor, and catharsis would deteriorate from their current condition of benign neglect to become an unabashed object of ridicule and hatred. The proposition that reading and writing will make you free somehow rings hollow when you force people, at the threat of their class status, to read and write the desires of a central committee.

If the best hope for the revival of the humanities is authoritarian coercion then perhaps it would be better just to let the whole thing go and focus the diminishing resources of the empire on improving science education by audiovisual means. We live in a time when more people, of their own volition, watch more drama, see more graphic art, and listen to more music than ever before. Culture's triumph over nature is so thorough that distinctions between rendering and model become more elusive all the time. Isn't there a way for humanists to appeal to the same energy that leads people to seek aesthetic experiences? American liberalism is based on the Enlightenment premise that if the understimulated masses of humanity were offered greater economic, educational, and artistic opportunities they would respond by recreating themselves into a meritocracy of ever more skillful and productive citizens. Instead we seem to have gotten a lot of people laying around in their underwear watching *Family Feud.*

Possible explanations:

1. Liberal. Television, despite its avant-garde distribution capability, is in a primitive a state of creative development and may one day yet contribute to a dynamic democratic age characterized by accessible information and culture; so let us have faith in PBS, Bravo, A&E, DSC, TLC, and pray.

2. Neoconservative. Television, because of its avant-garde distribution capability, evokes such great pressure for commercial usage that it can never be adequately shielded from the ravages of bland palatability; so let the urban peasants have their circuses while those of us with the adequate nature or nurture to survive the mass media push on with the great traditions of a usable past.

3. Techno-determinist. Television, which purveys valuable information and culture along with everything else that it purveys, shouldn't be blamed for the banal choices of the majority of its viewers or even the majority of its impresarios. Machines aren't stupid; people are. That is all.

4. Traditionalist conservative. Most people care little about aesthetic experience or the epic sense of history or anything in life that doesn't directly affect their immediate physical comfort and neither TV nor anything else under the sun is likely to change that.

Communists never came up with much of a position on TV and they have paid the price. As for Marxists, when was the last time you saw one on a talk show?

Marshall McLuhan, What Were You Doin'?

In *Marshall McLuhan: The Medium and the Messenger,* Philip Marchand carefully documents how McLuhan was encouraged to study the mass media not by wild-eyed radicals, but by establishment traditionalists at Cambridge University during the 1930s. F. R. Leavis, for example, specifically urged McLuhan to study billboard, magazine, and radio advertising, stressing the idea that it is a critic's duty to study the uses to which language is put, rather than to study books or any other particular medium per se. In their 1932 study, *Culture and Environment,* Leavis and his collaborator Denys Thompson had already recognized a shift in the center of the English language, which had been brought about in less than a decade by sound cinema and network radio.[15] Books were no longer the focal point of culture and communication, but rather an element in a larger media mix. "The more lasting effect of *Culture and Environment* on McLuhan," writes Marchand, "was its suggestion that practical literary criticism could be associated with training in awareness of the (media) environment." It was Leavis and Thompson's hope that "the analysis of prose and verse may be extended to the analysis of advertisements, the kind of appeal they make and their stylistic characteristics, followed up by comparison with representative passages of journalese and popular fiction."[16]

In a similar vein of thought, during the 1920s I. A. Richards had characterized the book as "a machine to think with," emphasizing that the product—thought—is of greater consequence than the instrument by which it is produced (i.e., the message is more important than the medium). According to Marchand, "In Richards' view, a poem is simply a supreme form of human communication. A reader analyzes a poem to see how it is able to achieve its effects—that is, to communicate an experience. English studies are themselves nothing but a study of the process of communication."[17] Writing the better part of a century ago Richards apparently had no problem in seeing reading and writing as a communication system. Most contemporary thinkers are not nearly so up-to-date. The book is put on a pedestal as white magic Art, while television, to name the salient example, is mistrusted as a black magic Communication system. "Art" and "Communication" are seen as separate, even unrelated subjects. Art stimulates the imagination by leading consciousness through metaphor; communication aborts imaginative capacity by handing down orders and flattering nitwits.

McLuhan, whose personal literary tastes ran toward the literary art of James Joyce and T. S. Eliot, wrote his doctoral thesis at Cambridge on the Elizabethan writer Thomas Nashe. Years later, asked why he had enlarged the focus of his work to encompass the mass communication media along with hightone Britlit, he replied, "I find most pop culture monstrous and sickening. I study it for my own survival."[18] If McLuhan's attitude became a fashion, the humanities might at least have a chance to go down swinging. But instead, there remains a terrible reluctance among professors without calculators to accept the fact that "high culture" and "popular culture" are components of a single mechanism and that this mechanism is manufacturing a society, from top to bottom, that everybody has to live in.

Some—the humanities faithful—believe that by ignoring crassly commercial or technologically complex forms they can give their energies to preserving a sacred flame of *Kultur* (and perhaps that their devotions will get them into secular humanist heaven). But this is an escapist fantasy that only serves to insulate the culture industry from the scrutiny of those with the most extraordinary potentials to understand it. Imagine how valuable a book *The Closing of the American Mind* might have been had Bloom saved his jeremiads for particular TV series or actual pieces of music instead of unloading all that nasty venom on the very existence of post-print technologies and genres, such as television and rock 'n' roll.[19]

Some others—the agnostics—accept a duty to examine TV shows, movies, government memoranda, baseball cards, or whatever, but only on the condition that they are recognized as white-gloved anthropological investigators visiting the artifacts of a culture that is foreign and distasteful to them. Todd Gitlin's *Inside Prime Time* (1984) is a powerful example of this self-serving stance. See especially the section on *Hill Street Blues* in that book. He, Todd Gitlin, Berkeley professor of sociology, former head of Students for a Democratic Society, almost gets carried away with his enthusiasm for a TV cop show. Oh my. But then, in the nick of time, he remembers he's a progressive intellectual and accuses television of capitalist brainwashing, thus saving his own gentility (and destroying the credibility of his previous critical commentary).

Whatever the subject matter, Jonathan Swift or Ninja Turtles, *Pamela* or *The Young and the Restless*, Alfred Steiglitz or *America's Funniest Home Videos*, the literacy charade continues as it must for the education industry to keep on cranking. The professors glance at their calendars, like Count Vlad taking a peak at the cross. The summer's almost over. They return from their vacations sometime around Labor Day and once again "ask" their nonreading and nonwriting students to read books and write about them. Perhaps the worst consequence of the spiritually based fixation of university education on reading and writing is that it prevents the true functions of literacy in the modern communications market from being determined. What does print actually do best? How can reading and writing be integrated into the emerging patterns of normal communication in contemporary society? We are not likely to find out if we keep making believe in school that literacy stands apart from, and above, all other forms of human communication.

There are those whose mystical belief in the written word is so powerful that they view the electronic media more as heresy than distraction. Neil Postman has made himself the best known of such critics. "Reading," he writes in *Amusing Ourselves to Death*, "is by its nature a serious business. It is also, of course, an essentially rational activity." Television, by contrast, he tells us, "promotes incoherence and triviality . . . the phrase 'serious television' is a contradiction in terms."[20] Television cannot teach us anything, but can only entertain. In this polar distinction he reasserts the Puritan belief that the very power to seduce indicates the presence of the devil.

I have to disagree. Television, like any transmission medium (including books) can dispense information to those who make the effort to receive it. To despise the quality of *what* we learn from television is a tacit admission that we are, in fact, learning. People who are incapable of writing a grammatical letter and who have never read a whole book can live reasonably prosperous and even relatively informed lives in the United States of America today. Is that a shame or a triumph? As for social maladjustment, it is more likely to be suffered by the intensely literate than by normal people.

Of course the best example to consult on the question of whether nonprint communication media are capable of teaching you anything, or of teaching you anything of worth, is yourself. Criticism without autobiography is too suspicious for words. At this point it is clear to me that I have learned most of what I know, if not necessarily the best of what I know, from watching TV. Though I took several college courses (which forced me to read books) pertaining to the causes and circumstances of World War II, I have no doubt that my major source of knowledge, certainly on the mechanics of the war—battles, military strategy, and so on—comes from having spent hundreds of hours watching commercial TV series such as *The World at War, Victory at Sea,* and *Prudential's The Twentieth Century.* Why did I watch these shows? Nobody told me to. I looked in the *TV Guide* (this learning took place in a preremote control environment) and picked them because I was interested in them. I can still see the swastikas sweeping out in all directions from the center of the map of Europe after the first commercial, scattering the union jacks, hammer-and-sickles, and tricolors into retreat until the stars-and-stripes arrive from the west, throwing the whole process into reverse. Television also gave me my first glance at the emaciated survivors and piles of corpses produced at Auschwitz and this of course was indispensable preparation for reading *The New York Review of Books.* As for what I know about the mating habits of kangaroos, gorillas, and penguins or of the ecological functions of rain forests and river basins, this is perhaps not enough, but virtually all of it can be directly attributed to TV nature programs. My imagination of the law and of courtroom procedures was formed by watching television series produced by Steven Bochco, such as *L.A. Law, Civil Wars,* and *NYPD Blue.* Should I have read law books instead? Middle-aged, quasi-embittered, and childless, the little I see of youth culture comes from channel-zapping tableaus of MTV.

I am fully aware that "admitting" these things may qualify me as an idiot in the eyes of book readers (and that of course is you; who else will ever process this data?). But let's drop the self-aggrandizing genteel bullshit and get serious for a minute. I've watched several hours of television every day for most of my life, and that adds up to tens of thousands of life-time hours in front of the set. Despite all that—to a large degree because of it—I've written this book and four others. In fact, I spend several hours writing almost every day. If this proves anything, it's that the two activities—literacy and television watching—are not mutually exclusive.

The search for disjunction between book-mind and TV-mind is not much of a search at all, but more like a ride in an air-conditioned car, windows up, through a wild animal theme park. It is so easy to ooh and ahh at the cultural monsters in their engineered environment. The search for continuities linking the two epistemological media is a trickier adventure. A book-made tendency to imagine the world as an accreting tale called history fights with a TV-made inclination to dig the juxtapositional incongruities of video montage. Book Head strives to understand the conflicting historical claims of Orthodox Serbia, Catholic Croatia and the Bosnian Muslims. TV Head experiences a flow of disgust at the wounded children and an ebb of ludicrous irony at the McDonald's commercial that follows it. Can history survive montage? Check your serotonin level and try segment three. Yes, you do have the attention span. I know you can do it.

1. Don DeLillo, *White Noise* (New York: Penguin, 1985), 51.

2. Ibid., 325–26.

3. Pazhitnov's game was programmed by Vadim Gerasimov. The version I play was adapted for Macintosh by Roland Gustafson and Sean Berger. Far more advanced versions of Tetris are now available but I have thus far avoided them out of fear.

4. Special note to book reviewers: If you've decided that you are against this book, attack me for committing the same crime against scholarship in the preceding section on *White Noise.*

5. Bernard Rosenberg and David Manning White, eds., *Mass Culture: The Popular Arts in America* (New York: Free Press, 1957). I highly recommend this book. It contains such classics of "the mass culture debate" as "A Theory of Mass Culture" by Dwight Macdonald and "The Public Arts" by Gilbert Seldes, as well as excerpts from writings on this subject by Whitman, de Tocqueville, Ortega, and others.

6. Robert Alter, *The Pleasures of Reading in an Ideological Age* (Simon and Schuster, 1989), 13.

7. Ibid., 12, 13.

8. See especially George Jackson, *Soledad Brother The Prison Letters of George Jackson* (New York: Coward-McCann, 1970) and Malcolm X with Alex Haley, *The Autobiography of Malcolm X* (New York: Grove Press, 1965).

9. Alter, 15.

10. Theodor W. Adorno, "Television and the Patterns of Mass Culture," *Quarterly of Film, Radio and Television* 8 (1954): 213.

11. I taught in the English Department at Wells College in 1981. Once the most popular major on that campus, English had dwindled to the point where only two of its offerings were literature courses; all the others were composition "service" courses. The most popular major on campus? Psychology.

12. This was true of the American Studies doctoral program at the University of Iowa, which I attended in the late 1970s.

13. Allan Bloom, *The Closing of the American Mind* (New York: Simon and Schuster, 1987), 60.

14. Ibid., 62.

15. The commercial release of *The Jazz Singer* by Warner Bros. and the launching of the NBC Red and Blue networks by RCA both occurred in 1927.

16. Philip Marchand, *Marshall McLuhan: The Medium and the Messenger* (New York: Ticknor and Fields, 1989), 35.

17. Ibid., 33.

18. Ibid., 43.

19. Actually, I would like to include more direct practical criticism of popular culture items, especially TV shows, in this book. But the editor won't let me.

20. Neil Postman, *Amusing Ourselves to Death* (New York: Viking, 1985), 50, 80.

"With mental automation as with physical automation there is an inevitable
transcendence of mere improvements in speed and efficiency."

Mass Memory
The Past in the Age of Television

As a technology devoted to a quick way for conveying whatever it has to say, TV has developed a remarkable visual cueing system for conjuring history. Take the last sixty years, for example: a cop smashes a beer barrel with an axe to the horror of frenzied flappers and a stockbroker leaps out the window of a Wall Street skyscraper; a factory gate slams shut on a crowd of unshaven men and Neville Chamberlain steps off an airplane triumphantly waving a piece of paper; Adolph Hitler rides in an open car through the Arc de Triomphe and a giant mushroom cloud forms over Hiroshima; a witness at a Senate hearing puts his hand over a microphone and a gigantic automobile stuffed with family members pulls into a suburban driveway; John F. Kennedy delivers the "ask not" line at his inauguration and hippies smoke pot, gyrate, and protest the Vietnam War; Nixon says good-bye and ducks into Air Force One and a line of cars stretches out into the street from a gas pump; a movie actor with a knowledge of history roughly equal to this paragraph delivers the "Are you better off?" line and a bomb armed with its own TV camera records its penetration of a Baghdad building.

And so what now? A teenaged pregnant woman smoking crack on a street corner as a thirty-eight-year-old man sits at a red light in a Lexus arguing with God knows who on a car phone? And so what now? America busily retooling for the coming wave of prosperity? America pathetically overspending what can be borrowed against past achievements in order to live in the style to which we have become accustomed? Enjoying the security of a world freed of the threat of nuclear war? Stockpiling weapons to defend ourselves against the psychological melt-downs of our neighbors?

History is memory, and memory—both the individual and collective

47

components of the process—has been undergoing a radical metamorphosis during the hundred years in which film, audiotape, videotape, and computers have joined the cave painting and the book as external vessels of recollection. The relationship between human memory and documentary communication media (or external memory) is often analogous to that of physical labor and machine automation.[1] In some cases the communication medium does no more than make easy what would otherwise be difficult. For example, take the case of a TV actor using a teleprompter or cue cards while speaking lines. The printed words, not visible to the audience, are used to promote the illusion that the actor is speaking from memory. And yet the memorization of lines, such as those a TV actor might deliver in the course of a broadcast, is not a feat that would necessarily stretch the capacity of the human mind; stage actors have been doing it for centuries. The written word, whether electronically generated or hand-printed, has merely reduced labor, in the same way that the use of a jackhammer can break up ten square feet of concrete with less human effort than if a pickaxe were employed.

But with mental automation as with physical automation, there is an inevitable transcendence of mere improvements in speed and efficiency. Capacities and propensities for entirely new operations emerge. The combined physical power of ten million slaves cannot hoist a rocket into outer space. By the same token it is one thing to memorize the Homeric epics and discuss them with others who have done likewise; it is quite another thing to have a library full of books at one's disposal that includes Homer's works annotated by dozens of readers from different centuries and differing cultures. That library is not only larger than one human memory or several, but it is qualitatively different. The print medium offers the reader an *Odyssey* that did not exist in a primarily oral culture.

Is all this to the reader's advantage? Certainly the necessity of memorizing poetry (and opinions about it) becomes less urgent as print "automates" the memorization process. As a direct result, the understanding of what poetry is—and what knowledge is—begins to shift. "An educated Greek was one who had *memorized* Homer, who could sing it or perform it [emphasis added]," Marshall McLuhan reminded his audiences. "He was a gentleman and a free man."[2] But in the age of books, the ability to recite became less important than the ability to cite.

In recent years the automation of memory has accelerated wildly, finding its way into the most intimate processes of thought and expression. For example, the word processing capacities of the personal computer with which I am writing this book offer the use of an internally imbedded thesaurus. Before I began writing with a word processor, I used to write with an electric typewriter. During that time I estimate that I used a thesaurus approximately once every fifty times I wrote or perhaps less than that. Now, with a "page" full of synonyms available at the touch of a fingertip, I tend to use the thesaurus as many as five or six times every time I write, compose, type, inscribe, scribble, doodle, jot, or scrawl. Has my vocabulary (i.e., language recall) improved because of this? Or has my vocabulary suffered because instead of searching my memory for synonyms, I have become dependent on an externalized automated memory, thus allowing my organic capacity for such mental work to atrophy? Similarly I used to know, by memory, the half dozen or so telephone numbers I dialed most often. Now these numbers are stored in the automatic dialing memory of my desk telephone and as a result I have forgotten most of them, forcing me to carry an address book or to call directory assistance when I need to make a call from an outside phone. Is this evidence that my memory is becoming more powerful?

The shifting (diminishing?) role of human memory in everyday life may provide clues to the stunning problems of shrinking attention span and lack of historical consciousness that seem to be plaguing education, and subsequently, the entire sphere of public life in America. Ideally the external mechanization of memory should be freeing human memory from busy work and trivia, producing greater opportunities for creative thought. But, in practice, is the automation of mundane recall activities obviating the very discipline that makes such vital creative activities as allusion, cross-referencing, suggestion, connotation, and implication possible?

Of all the communication media that are displacing, replacing, and redefining personal thought processes in the late twentieth century, none is more ubiquitous or potent than television. Above and beyond all of its functions, TV is a throbbing public memory. It continuously delivers and creates history in the form of the news; it continuously represents and interprets history in the form of dramatic programming. By manufacturing norms and by announcing the parameters of acceptable manners, styles, and language usage, it stimulates and constricts behavior, setting contexts and expectations for future events. As a first step in examining how television functions as an external cultural memory for its public, it is helpful to consider the place of television in a broader historical process: the extension of documented culture to the population at large, a process that has been occurring over the last three centuries.

In an essay written during the early years of network television, the critic Dwight Macdonald described pre-industrial Western civilization as the sum of two complementary cultural components: a *court culture* based on literacy and a *folk culture* based on oral communication.[3] In the former, human memory was externalized into bibliography. Religion, mathematics, documentation of events, criticism of the arts and sciences, and other ingredients in the production of consciousness were set into print impressions and stored in libraries. Access to these data banks was limited to a tiny, genetically determined user group of aristocratic and clerical readers. The medieval library can be imagined as a vast pre-electronic computer, with human beings moving through its corridors, retrieving units of information and carrying them to desktops for human perusal, a job since automated to electronic impulses.

In the case of the vast nonliterate majority, stories, beliefs, and skills were passed on by word of mouth in a system of integral kinship relationships. For those who could not read, memory remained essentially an organic (that is, nonautomated) process. According to Macdonald, the two subcultures, court and folk, peacefully coexisted, aware of each other, but without designs of conquest.

The ruling courts aggrandized their culture through the establishment of institutions such as universities, academies, libraries, and museums, which in turn celebrated certain authors and artists as geniuses and heroes, certain works as masterpieces, and certain media and genres as inherently superior to others. An accreting history, or cultural memory, was thus written and preserved as "the great tradition" of a society, or *Kultur* as denoted in German. As bookmaking technology progressed, the primarily oral character of traditional courtly forms, such as classical epic poetry and Renaissance stage drama, receded from cultural memory; poems and plays were documented in ink and introduced to generations of readers as print phenomena.[4] The longer-than-life endurance of books became a key element in establishing the rhetorical hegemony of what later came to be known as "high culture." By contrast, folk culture was artifactual and phenomenal, lacking verifiable or authentic texts, lacking the signatures of geniuses and lacking clearly definable lines of rational evolutionary development.

These two socially determined constituents of feudal culture were not of course completely autonomous from each other. To name the primary exception, the matter of religion was dictated to the folk by the court, at the threat of military force if necessary. This was particularly important because religious belief was—and some argue still is—a basic source for all cultural expression.[5] The medieval cathedral functioned as an important cultural bridging phenomenon between the elite and the folk, acting as a communication medium for the translation of the Bible and other religious messages into nonliterate forms such as sculpture, painting, and stained glass. The cathedral also functioned, by means of its lavish architecture, as a symbol to the peasantry of the temporal power of the reader-builders.

Given the significant prescription of religion, folk cultures were able to maintain some degree of lateral independence from the court. Though unsigned by their illiterate *auteurs*, tales, songs, visual designs, medical remedies, and other cultural items were created, distributed, and retained in a nonliterate system of learning and remembrance. With the advent of industrialization, however, this bilateral model of culture described by Macdonald gradually disintegrated. The horizontal communication system of class equals passing on culture to class equals, both at court and on the back forty, was replaced by a vertical model that Macdonald and other twentieth-century commentators called "mass culture." Under these new conditions an educated elite of cultural specialists developed. It was their task to create culture—at first in print, but later by whatever means available—to be sold at market to the newly literate urban classes. In *Literature in the Marketplace*, Per Gedin writes

> During the eighteenth century the foundations were laid for what was later to be called 'the reading public.' The invention of the printing press in the fifteenth century provided the technical precondition for a much wider dispersal of the written word, but it was not until the period of blossoming capitalism in the eighteenth century that the aristocracy's exclusive privilege of education was broken. . . . The reading public developed initially through the publication of newspapers and magazines.[6]

Some hoped that the introduction of literacy to previously excluded classes would result in a general sharing of what had once been the finest of the culture of the few. In *Culture and Anarchy*, Matthew Arnold expressed the hopeful thought that "the sweetness and light of the few must be imperfect until the raw and unkindled masses of humanity are touched with sweetness and light."[7] It soon became obvious, however, that publishing-for-profit would reshape and redefine culture rather than simply distribute it more widely. Arnold never bargained for the bitterness and darkness of *The National Enquirer* or *Geraldo*.

A new culture of inexpensive periodicals and books went on sale. But what memory did this culture have to draw upon for its rhetoric, its metaphors, its vision of order, or its senses of the comic and the tragic?[8] What versions of etiology and history might give it coherence? Here was an expanding audience that had been trained to read, but had not been *educated* by any previous standard. Here was an audience that could read, but could not read classical Greek or Latin. Would or could the nascent reading classes adopt or accept the historical memory that had been developed by (and for) aristocratic readers over the ages? Might adaptations of oral folkways find their way into the print world to merge with an aristocratic world view? The progressives of the reading societies advocated the former; romantic poets, notably Wordsworth, dreamed of the latter.[9] While a bit of both did occur, the result is better described as a *tertium quid;* new memories—what might be called mass memories—were forged for a new culture: mass culture.

A contest for public memory took place in the book stalls that began sprouting in cities of readers during the eighteenth century. A prevailing recollective paradigm emerged that would remain at the heart of European politics and culture for most of the next two centuries. Thomas Paine, Karl Marx, Émile Zola, and the other writers who founded what eventually came to be known as the political Left posited an historical memory dominated by economic relations and, quite specifically, by the mechanics of economic exploitation. Pamphlets, newspapers, novels, plays, and other texts from the emerging Left subculture told the new class of urban workers that they could achieve consciousness (i.e., a grasp on reality, a sense of coherence) by *remembering* that throughout history it was their own toil and the toil of those like them that had laid the foundation upon which all human achievement had been built. Their struggle for food, clothing, and shelter was valorized as the salient feature of the past and the recollection of it empowered them in an ongoing struggle to throw off the yoke of their exploiters. This heritage of economic exploitation provided a moral mandate for the seizure of political power, a revolution that in any case was bound to take place as the evolving nature of work required ever increasing degrees of education among workers. The Revolution of 1917 institutionalized class memory as official history in Russia and in the republics and parties throughout the world that belonged to or supported the old Soviet Union.

Right-wing response, epitomized in the work of such commentators as Arthur Gobineau, José Ortega y Gasset, and various geneticists and social Darwinists, rejected the heritage of class conflict and instead promoted racial and ethnic memory.[10] The granting of literacy, suffrage, and other cultural rights to the lower classes necessitated a theory of justification for continuing upper-class privilege. To this end, the past was recuperated chiefly in tribal terms. Genetic purity was publicly recalled as an Edenic condition of communal harmony. Evil, usually associated with disorder, could not be traced to an internal exploitative class structure, but rather to the introduction of unwholesome exogenous genetic forces. In ethnically cantonized Europe, the chief historical villains in this scenario were the Jews, portrayed as a racially identifiable minority from another continent who had penetrated the national *bund*. Gypsies and other submerged or displaced minorities, such as the Anatolian Greeks of Turkey, also fit the bill in this regard. Entire European political parties were founded on anti-Semitic and other types of xenophobic platforms, culminating in the election to power of the National Socialists in Germany in 1933 and the subsequent establishment of fascist parties and states throughout Europe in the decade that followed.

Totalitarians of all stripes were particularly keen to use the new electronic communications media to promote or create official cultural memories for their populations. The propaganda films of Eisenstein and Reifenstel as well as the radio addresses of Hitler and Mussolini are all artifacts of the belief that these new media could be used efficiently as direct instruments for the inculcation of collective memory. The ideological distinctions between communist and fascist memory lessons grew increasingly elusive with the passage of time. By the 1980s the Stalinist regime of Bulgaria was carrying on an "ethnic cleansing" campaign that required all citizens of Turkic ancestry to change their surnames to Slavic-sounding analogues.[11]

The sudden and utter ruin of European Communism in the late 1980s, and the overnight outbreak of ethnic animosities and wars that ensued, signaled a decisive end to the rhetorical peculiarities of the Left-Right battle for the past. In his book *The Consciousness Industry* (1974), Hans Magnus Enzensberger was among the first to look beyond this collapsing paradigm to describe a new set of conditions for the character and role of public memory in the age of television. Though written before the end of the Vietnam-Afghanistan climax, this book reads like a political wake-up call from the Psychic Friends Network.

First of all, though perhaps least dazzling, Enzensberger argues that the grand opposition between "High Culture" and "Low Culture," once a germinating center of Western intellectual discourse, has actually shriveled in significance. Despite the need of many intellectuals—veterans of both sides of the Left-Right wars—to hang on to a concept that honors their own taste above that of nonprofessionals, the terms "high" and "low" now chiefly refer to demographic marketing niches.

Culture today is produced and distributed by a very few corporations, which, through their many divisions and subsidiaries, make decisions about what culture all members of society will consume, from the top of the social ladder to the bottom. So, this logic goes, General Electric, Murdoch's News Corporation, Time-Warner, CBS, the Bertelsmann Group, and other giant media conglomerates share a collective stake in presenting their publics with cultural items spawned by coherent cultural flows (or what used to be called "cultural traditions"). These corporations talk to various segments of the public-cum-audience over broadcast networks, cable networks, printed matter, audio recordings, and combinations of media. But corporations produce and distribute memory and thus regulate consciousness. Just as the garment industry reaches both high and low, from exclusive boutiques to schlocky discount stores, so has the consciousness industry achieved a comprehensive industrial oligarchy over culture at large through the domination of memory distribution.

Enzensberger builds this broad and general analysis upon a very personal, and in some ways shocking, foundation of individual experience. He reflects on how we *like to think* that "we reign supreme in our own consciousness, that we are masters of what our minds accept or reject," that each mind is a kind of "last refuge" where the individual is still in charge of self. But this, he tells us, is an illusion. The belief in self-autonomy, where such belief still exists, is a vain faith in what he dismisses as an "imaginary fortress."[12] Unfortunately, we can no longer think of our minds as our own because mass culture, with its endless barrage of styles, suggestions, moral codes, and so on, has become the context for all of our thinking. Even to count oneself in opposition to mass culture is to participate in it. Mass culture requires an opposition to ornament its legitimacy.

This kind of atmospheric penetration of consciousness is different from the time-honored idea that "what is going in our minds . . . is a product of society."[13] It is more insidious. When communication was mostly oral and personal there was room enough and time for the individual to make decisions about what to accept and what not to accept. Learning relationships such as student and teacher, apprentice and master, and congregant and clergyman, were human relationships in which the character of the teacher could be measured against the content of the lesson. Given the nature of contemporary education—given class size alone—such relationships are rarely possible in schools today. More to the point, the information gained in schools becomes a shrinking percentage of the whole as increasing quantities of data are industrially distributed by mass media, a situation in which interpersonal relationships are rendered structurally impossible. The transmissions of billboards, tee-shirts, radios, and television screens are, alternately and simultaneously, bits of two-dimensional wallpaper *and* piercing missiles of data, toggling significances, shifting in relation to the murky rhythms of personal psychological predisposition.[14] McLuhan coined the term "sobconscious inklings" to describe this phenomenon.

The job of passing information, an act essential to the creation of individual consciousness, has been given over to what Enzensberger calls "the mind-making industry." Furthermore, he warns us that the character of this revolutionary system is largely invisible, especially to students of modern culture who are still wed to the ideological templates of the past:

> It (the consciousness industry) has developed at such a pace and assumed such varied forms that it has outgrown our understanding and our control. Our current discussion of the media seems to suffer from severe theoretical limitations. Newspapers, films, television, public relations tend to be evaluated separately, in terms of their specific technologies, conditions, and possibilities. . . . Hardly anyone seems to be aware of the phenomenon as a whole.[15]

The political imagination that evolved out of the Left-Right paradigm created a vision of a power elite that uses the communication media to organize or even hypnotize people by repeatedly feeding them predigested messages that will lead them to predesired behaviors. When necessary, deviance is dealt with by secret police, as in Orwell's *1984*. In another variation of this theme, drugs are used as less obviously violent persuaders, as in Huxley's *Brave New World*.[16]

But Enzensberger paints a different picture of how communications media are actually used to rule a society. The media machines—in the form of TV, radio, movie projector, printing press—are indeed spitting out the data, but the success of the system is dependent on its ability to persuade the public to collaborate with it in the creation of a social product. Every time we dress in a certain style that we have learned (or learned to admire) from the mass media, we are socially legitimating another small piece of data to the people around us who respect us, look up to us, depend on us, are attracted to us, envy us and so on. In this way that particular piece of information emerges from the clutter to significance. At the same time, the echo of a more personal folk system warms and lubricates the distribution of these messages. An aesthetic crevice for personal taste is maintained.

The old book-made image of a one-way stream of electronically generated data simply filling up millions of blank minds made for an easy villain; the transmitter of data was guilty. The Left blamed big business; the Right, big government. But where actually tried, this totalitarian model has proved more or less unworkable, especially as mini-communicators—photocopiers, FAX machines, personal computers and so on—allowed significant numbers of people to become franchised consciousness distributors. If we accept Enzensberger's model, we might imagine an entire population milling around a smorgasbord of suggestions, tasting, sampling, and recommending the fare to each other. The caterer, the supplier of the food, hardly seems like a villain.

In the advanced capitalist countries—the United States, Canada, Japan, and the nations of Western Europe—the culture industry is not so much charged with the duty of initiating ideas as with testing their viability as attractive products. Thus if a garage band comes up with a new pop sound or a TV producer comes up with a new wrinkle in a formula drama, the task of the vast entertainment-industrial complex is not so much to evaluate the quality or the lack of quality of this invention, or its beauty or truth or lack of same, but rather to test how deeply it can penetrate the market without causing disruption of the marketplace. Demography becomes more important than either democracy or autocracy. If those owning the means of communication know who you are, they can make you love them.

The same holds true in terms of collective historical memory. Writing about such media-staged events as the Statue of Liberty centennial and the bicentennial of the U.S. Constitution, Susan G. Davis commented, "the way we experience the past and present, the very experience we have to interpret, is being rebuilt for us through marketing strategies." [17] By turning these historical memorials into corporately sponsored television programs, the selling of soft drinks, automobiles, and toothpaste is put on an equal footing with the events themselves. The Constitution guarantees the spectator's freedom of speech; Coca Cola quenches the spectator's thirst.

In societies still wed to older ideological templates such as Deng Xiaoping's China and Saddam Hussein's Iraq the role of the mind industry is less subtle. Straightforward political propaganda is still commonplace. Politics is treated as if it were simply a matter of taking sides. In such societies it becomes the job of the elite to inform the mass audience as to which opinions it must subscribe to and to warn individuals of the consequences of failing to take the government-sponsored side.

But in both parliamentary democracies and authoritarian societies the mass media are of equal importance to the degree that systemic power has become a matter of information. Individual survival becomes dependent on the receipt of information. In the eighteenth century, if a revolution was to be successful it had to seize control of the royal palace, as in the taking of Versailles in the French Revolution. In the nineteenth century, if a revolution was to be successful, it had to take the center of the capital city with its factories and great public squares, as in the national revolutions of 1848. But in the twentieth century, the revolutionaries must take the TV station to make a credible seizure of power.

Imagine an anchorman in military uniform appearing on CNN one evening. He greets the audience, proclaims himself the new president of the United States and offers a list of reasons for deposing the elected president. Would the viewer scoff at this as nonsense, or would the very fact that this person is appearing on television lend credence to his claim? Indeed, wouldn't the burden of proof fall on the elected government to demonstrate that a coup had *not* taken place? What strategy might the elected government choose to attempt to reassert itself? It would have to "take back" CNN (for Ted Turner or perhaps away from him) or make convincing counterbroadcasts over other networks. The technological miracle of international satellite transmission attests to the power of those who can manipulate it, just as the building of the cathedral and the publishing of the book did in former ages.

Of course such shocking announcements of new realities are rare on television, especially in nontotalitarian states, where TV is far more concerned with the business of continuity than the antibusiness atmosphere engendered by disruption. The medium is most effective when it is integrating change into a seamless flow of consciousness, shaping and evolving a public sphere for the reception of new data. Enzensberger calls the training of populations to use television this way "the industrialization of the mind." He sets down four prerequisites for rule by media to take place in a society, paraphrased here.

The first of these is the successful selling of the idea that intellectual enlightenment is the highest form of human achievement. Because TV is usually associated with a body of rhetoric ranging from the simplistic to the moronic, this observation may seem mischievous or even senseless at first. But recognition of the cultural mechanism that it implies is essential to understanding the power of television as a communication system. People must be convinced that improvement of their life comes not from some invisible force (such as God or spiritual principles), but out of a TV set or other such tangible receiving and playback devices.

In a society where theocracy rules or maintains a large organized following, the consciousness industry is limited in its power. States that officially subscribe to, or people who sincerely believe in sacred books or in the presence of supernatural forces are less susceptible to electronic media manipulation. Interestingly, television programs often pay lip service to the virtues of traditional religion. But the concerns of religion are of only marginal significance in TV content compared to secular messages about consumption. Which is of greater value, smelling good or cleansing the soul? Dressing in style or going to heaven? Fear of sexual rejection or fear of God? Television and the cultural order it advertises must establish itself with the audience as a more highly valued guide to successful living than the messages printed in the Bible or spoken from the pulpit, even the electronic pulpit. Television has presented its audience with an emphatically secular vision, offering immediate tangible results and rarely dwelling on what Victor Lidz called "the problem of eternity."[18]

Enzensberger's identification of traditional religious faith as the chief antagonist of mass media culture has proved particularly prescient since he offered it some twenty years ago. The most serious political challenges to consumption-oriented media rule have indeed come from theocratically inspired forces. Examples include the revolution in Iran and the rise of religious fundamentalism in several regions of the Islamic world, the renaissance of fundamentalist Protestantism in the United States and even in the power of the Orthodox Jewish right wing in Israeli politics. Though each of these political movements was spawned from a distinct religious tradition, each is committed to an attempt to roll back what it has defined as the secular, materialist juggernaut of electronic media influence, and to reassert the power of religion and religious leaders in everyday life. Socialist attacks on "consumerism" or on the "capitalist content" of mass culture have provoked far less interest from the public.

The second prerequisite is a proclamation of equality and human rights as official rhetoric, no matter what the reality is. In Western Europe, the touchstone of official freedom is the French Revolution; in the former Communist countries it is the Bolshevik Revolution of 1917; in the Americas, Africa, and Asia, it is the revolts that ended colonial subjugation. Whether people actually have these rights or not becomes less significant than whether they are willing to accept as "fact" the proposition that they have been guaranteed these rights through a verified historical event. In terms of collective memory, this is the most important of Enzensberger's preconditions. The past must provide a structure that makes revolutionary challenge obsolete or, better yet, absurd. The Soviet practice of committing dissenters to mental hospitals spoke directly to this last point.

Thus television comes upon the scene as a post-revolutionary apparatus for the implementation of consensual utopian ideals: the sharing of prosperity that is manifest in the offering of consumer goods to all who view, the exercise of freedom manifest in choosing among consumer objects, and the availability of credit to ensure democratic participation and gratification. Which kind of information is more highly prized: how to get a BMW or how to achieve eternal salvation? Theological concerns are marginalized in a consciousness overwhelmed with practical suggestions for getting ahead.

The third prerequisite is a measure of economic prosperity in the society. The growl of a hungry stomach is still loud enough to distract a viewer from television, no matter how hypnotic the effect of the medium is imagined to be. What is more important, the ruling elite of such a society is well aware that it would be necessary to use old-fashioned force to put down a hungry population. The behavior of the hungry or of the cold is difficult or even impossible to manipulate with symbols. Avoidance of that kind of messy public violence is among the chief advantages to governance by media. This is also a reminder that media dominance is not possible in just any society. It implies an evolutionary course of national development that must be reached for it to occur.

The fourth prerequisite is the existence of the proper technology to invade every facet of life with electronic messages. This fourth prerequisite is related to the third. If people don't have electricity and radios and TV sets, they cannot be manipulated by electronic media. In addition to the availability of subsistence goods and consumer goods, there must be an acceptance of consumerism as a way of life, which is not always quite so forthcoming as it may seem. This was even evident in the United States during the 1950s, as the nation was emerging from a prolonged period of economic hardship and war to become the world's first TV-dominated consumer society. Marketing specialist Ernest Dichter, facing this dilemma, was moved to comment that "one of the basic problems of this prosperity is to give people the sanction and justification to enjoy it and to demonstrate that the hedonistic approach to life is a moral one, not an immoral one."[19] Once again, the Bible, though touted for its wisdom when the subject comes up in sitcoms and made-for-TV movies, can be quite unfavorable to this kind of thinking.

Print plays a role in mass-mediated society but only a limited one. During the period when its chief rival as a social memory system was orality, print was a technologically advanced medium, the medium of choice for those with the skills to use it. In terms of late twentieth-century technology, however, print proves relatively slow and inefficient. As I have attempted to demonstrate, the special conditions for accessing print—especially quiet and long periods of uninterrupted time—are increasingly elusive. Machines that are quicker and less vulnerable to immediate conditions have pushed literacy to a medium of late resort. How many letters have not been written because of the telephone? How many novels have not been read because of the cinema? How many newspapers have folded since the establishment of the network television system in the late 1940s? How many "how to" manuals have been bypassed in favor of videotapes? How much reading time on trains and buses has been sacrificed to the car stereo and to looking out the window? How much reading time on airplanes has been lost to in-flight motion pictures? How much time does the poetry of the video game leave for the poetry of poetry?

It seems that in every instance where print has been forced to compete with electronic audiovisual media in an open communications market it has gone into retreat. The great exception of course is the schools, where print continues to dominate by means of official fiat. Yet teachers somehow continue to wonder why so many of their students have such difficulty reading and writing. As early as 1964 Marshall McLuhan provided a clue to that mystery when he observed that children raised with television "bring to print all their senses, and print rejects them. Print asks for the isolated and stripped-down visual faculty, not for the unified sensorium."[20]

If, as McLuhan implies, the synaesthetic pleasure of multimedia experience is by its very nature more attractive than the single-sense visual focus of reading, what are the consequences for human memory? For one thing, visceral reaction takes priority over the particulars of content in personal recall and this is inimical to the inculcation of cultural memory in the traditional sense. Images, styles, tones, fashions, ambiences, and manners are salient. Facts, dates, names, places, institutions, cause-and-effect theories and other components that inform a literacy-based historical perspective are reduced to the accoutrements of an entertainment experience.[21]

Unless the viewer chooses to pause the electronic feed and to write these things down, thus introducing and synthesizing print into the audiovisual communication process, the details necessary for reasoned argument pass by at a rhythm unimpeded by the rate or depth of the viewer's comprehension. Even when stored on videotape, factual data is extremely difficult to access. If in doubt, compare searching through the pages of a book, with its static text and its index and table of contents, to fast-forward and fast-rewind searching on a VCR in pursuit of a piece of information.[22]

In his moving study, *Time Passages: Collective Memory and Popular Culture*, George Lipsitz finds the relationship between a personal sense of history and the electronic media "paradoxical." He observes that

> time, history and memory become qualitatively different concepts in a world were electronic mass communication is possible. Instead of relating to the past through a shared sense of place or ancestry, consumers . . . can experience a common heritage with people they have never seen; they can acquire memories of a past to which they have no geographic or biological connection. This capacity . . . to transcend time and space creates instability by disconnecting people from past traditions, but it also liberates people by making the past less determinate of experiences in the present.[23]

Lipsitz's ambiguity goes to the heart of the matter. On the dark side, he sees the mass media as having atomized people from organic kinship relationships. Even McLuhan's celebrated 1960s image of a family gathered around the "electric hearth" seems warm and quaint today when measured against the reality of demographically balkanized family members moving to their personal TV sets at separate corners of the home in the age of wide-spectrum cable targeting.

Barry Levinson's 1990 film, *Avalon,* is a powerful statement of the pessimistic view. Through most of the film an immigrant grandfather functions as a household shaman, telling and retelling stories of the family's American origins at the turn of the century. When television arrives at the house, however, he is gradually supplanted from this position. The final scene of the film takes place in a nursing home where the grandfather now lives. His son brings his young grandson to visit him on Thanksgiving Day, hoping that the old man will retell the story of his coming to America, as had been the family custom on that holiday for decades. Indeed the grandfather, despite his enfeeblement, begins to spin the magic tale, but it simply does not get the grandson's attention. The television is going, as indeed it always is at such institutions, and the boy is fixed on the Macy's Thanksgiving Day Parade, a commercial event that is no way connected to the original meaning of the holiday or to its special meaning for his family. How can the words of an old man compete with the audiovisual allure of marching bands and skyscraper-size cartoon characters?

The optimistic scenario that Lipsitz suggests, that mass-media dominance will release people from the bigotries and parochialisms that are passed from one generation to the next, is perhaps something more than a pipe dream but less than a redemptive hope for the future of the human race. Despite the complicity of the audience, as described by Enzensberger, it does not appear at this stage of development that the vertical system of culture made possible by mass communications technology can fulfill the biologically based emotional needs of the atomized member of the audience. The chronic epidemic of clinical depression, the rising rates of murder, suicide, and random violence, the now protracted threats to the family of divorce and child abandonment, the appearance of whole new psychosomatic ailments (notably Epstein-Barr Syndrome) are evidence of a population that has been disconnected from the roots of its organic capacity to remember: to recall, to re-experience, to recuperate, to re-create itself.[24] Though often and carelessly blamed for society's ills, television and other mass communications media are surely symptoms of this disconnectedness, though not necessarily causes.

And so we sit, remote control in hand, a fifty-channel spectrum to graze, shelves full of videotapes, AM and FM, CD player, tape deck, phonograph, telephone, FAX machine, waiting for virtual reality, searching for something to remember, nothing particular to forget.

1. Most communication media are documentary, in that they process messages into replayable, reproduceable documents. Print, film, audiotape, videotape, and computer discs all fit this description. Not all media belong in this category, however. The telephone, for example, is not by itself a documentary medium.

2. Stephanie McLuhan, prod., *Marshall McLuhan: The Man and His Message* by Tom Wolfe. Canadian Broadcasting Company, 1984. Cheap printing and widespread literacy have turned books into a mass-communication medium over the last two hundred years. As a result, generations of students have been asked to read print documentations of stage plays that were originally written by Shakespeare for audiovisual presentation. Some readers of these books have only rarely seen a Shakespeare play produced on stage; others never at all. In any case, their understanding of what Shakespeare did must differ radically from the playwright's contemporary audience.

3. Dwight Macdonald, "A Theory of Mass Culture" (1953). Reprinted in *Mass Culture: The Popular Arts in America*, ed. Bernard Rosenberg and David Manning White (New York: Free Press, 1957), 60.

4. The career of Alexander Pope exemplifies the direction of Western high culture during the eighteenth century in this regard. Pope translated Greek and Latin poetry for English publication and edited a new edition of Shakespeare's plays. Moreover, as a poet, he employed the rhyming heroic couplet, a quintessentially oral line, in works designed specifically for print.

5. T. S. Eliot argues the continuing significance of this point in the twentieth century in his 1948 essay "Notes Toward the Definition of Culture," in *Christianity and Culture* (New York: Harcourt, 1968), 79–202.

6. Per Gedin, *Literature in the Marketplace*, trans. George Bisset (Woodstock, N.Y.: The Overlook Press, 1977), 13.

7. Matthew Arnold, *Culture and Anarchy*. (1869; reprint, J. Dover Wilson, ed. London: Cambridge Univ. Press, 1950), 69.

8. Pope was a merciless critic of this bargain basement literacy in such poems as "The Dunciad" and "An Essay on Criticism."

9. Wordsworth's "Preface to the Lyrical Ballads" published in 1801, is a kind of manifesto for an inclusionary aesthetic that would synthesize courtly form with folkish content in a language available to all classes of English readers.

10. A classic statement of this position is Arthur Gobineau's "Essay on the Inequality of Races" (1870), in *Arthur Gabineau: Selected Political Writings*, ed. Michael D. Biddis (New York: Harper and Row, 1970).

11. For more information on the Bulgarian government's violent, often fatal, anti-Turkic campaign, see *The New York Times*. Front page articles covering the campaign appeared in the *Times* on January 17, February 7, and February 8, 1985.

12. Han Magnus Enzensberger, *The Consciousness Industry* (New York: Seabury, 1974), 3.

13. Ibid.

14. DeLillo's *White Noise*, cited in Segment 1, is a masterful depiction of this phenomenon.

15. Enzenberger, *Consciousness Industry*, 4.

16. See Neil Postman, *Amusing Ourselves to Death* (New York: Viking, 1985), vii.

17. As quoted in Michael Kammen, *Mystic Chords of Memory* (New York: Knopf, 1991), 669.

18. Victor Lidz, "Television and Moral Order in a Secular Age," in *Media in Society: Readings in Mass Communication*, ed. Caren J. Deming and Samuel L. Becker (Glenview, Ill.: Scott Foresman, 1988), 55.

19. George Lipsitz, *Time Passages: Collective Memory and American Popular Culture* (Minneapolis: Univ. of Minnesota Press, 1990), 47.

20. Marshall McLuhan, *Understanding Media* (New York: Signet, 1964), 269.

21. For a somewhat hyperbolic but nevertheless consistent presentation of this argument see Postman, *Amusing Ourselves to Death*.

22. It is worth noting that this problem is being addressed in newer audiovisual technology, such as CD-ROM and the video laser disc, which digitalize content and provide a printed table of contents, thus making each information bit in the text more easily accessible, "like a book."

23. Lipsitz, *Time Passages*, viii.

24. According to the *University of California at Berkeley Wellness Letter*, 9 (Oct. 1992), 4, "Nearly 10 million Americans sought help from psychiatrists, psychologists, social workers, or hospital psychiatric clinics in 1980, the first year such a count was taken. If visits to counselors, specialists in geriatric problems and such support groups as Alcoholics Anonymous, not to mention conversations with . . . (clergy) . . . were added to the count, this total might easily double."

"A lack of blueprints has turned the would-be architects of a new world
into a bunch of home improvement amateurs."

Culture Without Context

The dissipation of historically based left-wing–right-wing bipolarities for political, cultural, and moral thinking has created a structural gap in the perceptual processes of book-trained people. This gap, this emptiness, this yawning black hole in the data-processing capacities of the post-modern intelligentsia is an adrenalizing stimulant to the hysteria that currently grips the tweeny-weeny demographic segment of active literati. For centuries, print thinking has been organized upon the foundation of a "nurture or nature" debate. Can humanity be improved by a willful elite that can define improvement and remain dedicated to its implementation? Or are people prisoners of chromosomal configurations, acting out encoded programs, helpless to significantly affect their fates? Marxism and geneticism, the two precipitates of this paradigm, constitute the definitive legacy of the book world. As it happens, neither of these "big ideas" plays well on television.

Whether seen as endlessly betrayed true-believer revolutionaries or as bureaucrats structurally incapable of delivering toilet paper and blue jeans, Marxists have not so much been defeated in TV-land as cancelled, losers in a ratings struggle no matter what the theoretical virtues or shortcomings of their program. Without Marxism, progressive idealists have been deprived of a standard of progress; more important, perhaps, they no longer even have a standard by which to measure their own martyrdom or sense of betrayal (i.e., the Soviet Union). A lack of blue-prints has turned the would-be architects of a new world into a bunch of home-improvement amateurs. International worker movements yield to parlor room "political correctness" sessions.

Geneticism, like Marxism, is a comprehensive template that restores sensible literary order to post-Christian phenomenological chaos, lending the harmony of tribal hierarchy to the relentless barrage of data that comes spewing forth from the communication machines. But it too has problems with telegenic appeal. Like most kinds of determinist thinking, geneticism is antithetical to consumerism. Mass culture is, along with all its other qualities, an inclusivist ideology, seeking room in its big tent for every social security number capable of handling a dollar. Advertising has a firm and unwavering commitment to a decisive transcendence of the individual's current place in the world through the action of buying. In this way media-directed consumption directly opposes the fundamental tenets of most religions, which focus on building satisfaction that can tolerate or even celebrate material scarcity.

Geneticism hardly ever figures in the plot resolutions of TV dramas. When it does play on the tube, it tends to come out as pure and simple racism, the mandate for the dress-up queens of the Ku Klux Klan and the Aryan People's Nation, or the philosophical touchstone for the separatist rage of a Meyer Kahane or a Louis Farahkan. Denied respectable public expression of their "scientific" genetic assumptions, many social Darwinist conservatives feel deprived of their most precious private property. They save their resentment for the "politically correct" liberals whose self-aggrandizing idealism has blinded them to the obvious truths of a DNA-based understanding of life.

Left or Right, few book-trained thinkers outside of the commercial communications industry are prepared to accept the spectacle of consumerism as a faith that has outstripped both socialism and tribalism, that its oracle is television and that the purchasing of material objects will suffice for most congregants in terms of transcendental, utopian, or practical organizational experience. Of all the depressing and repulsive intellectual consequences traceable to the cerebral panic over the Left-Right meltdown, the most bothersome manifests itself as political correctness, a rhetorical bad penny whose moral grime attracts the dislocated attention spans of book-world intellectuals attempting to prove their immunity to the mass culture that has shaped society. The very words "political correctness" strike terror in the heart of any one who reads books or who watches political talk shows in search of some sensible or engaging discourse that might qualify as a contemporary descendant of what used to be known as belles lettres. Smug conservatives mask racist, sexist, and homophobic prejudices with tales of how they are being persecuted by a powerful cabal of Perrier-swigging social engineers. Self-righteous liberals mask their hypocritical distrust of constitutional democracy by treating freedom of speech as if it were an abstract painting the true meaning of which was obvious only to aesthetes such as themselves.

The producers of American commercial popular culture have always sought to detach moral questions from their political and cultural contexts. Just watch a few dozen hours of TV and you will receive scores of lessons about right and wrong, but very little information about politics, religion, love, or history. The same is true of a political correctness discussion. As both practice and controversy, these discussions are the waste product of a generation of intellectuals whose aim—whose raison d'etre—is to prove the depth of its alienation from popular thinking. Lefties and Righties have collaborated to adapt the centuries-old literary debate over the relationship of individual freedom to the state into a screaming sitcom in which the quantity and speed of one-liners takes precedence over the moral implications of the drama.

Writing about this subject without taking an easy to understand "us-against-them" position, one way or the other, is a no-win situation for a writer. The bipolar reflex is immediately stimulated by the subject. People on the Hillary side of Bill Clinton are bewildered, even offended, by anyone who would give aid and comfort to the enemies of peace and love by admitting that political correctness is anything more than a figment of Pat Buchanan's paranoid imagination. Similarly, the few conservatives I know who are willing to talk to an alleged pot-smoking homosexual such as myself (and believe me, "alleged" is the key word), although thrilled by the prospect of a walking, talking stereotype such as yours truly complaining about p.c. brutality, somehow can't believe that I'd ruin the whole thing by including apologia for the sins of these two-bit academic Stalins. How queer!

In any case, the events you are about to encounter are true. The names have been omitted to protect my next job search.

What Is Political Correctness?

Political correctness is, in theory, an attempt to avoid or to break out of certain conventional traps of language that cause speakers and writers to collaborate in the perpetuation of stereotypes that deny the humanity of individuals. In practice, however, political correctness is at least as often a parlor demonstration staged by emphatically educated people who are moved to prove that they are holier-than-thou, or anyone else for that matter, because of the unbearable sensitivities afforded them by their bloated consciousnesses. All of this could be dismissed as just another case of good old-fashioned idealism deteriorating into boring old-fashioned pedantry, except for one thing: self-righteous intolerance of intolerance is being taken seriously enough to spawn a tolerance for speech codes on college campuses and at other places where it is best to err on the side of freedom. This is a particularly dangerous erosion of civil liberties in that developing generations of Americans may take it increasingly for granted that people in authority have a natural right, or worse yet, a duty, to regulate the vocabulary of others.

Though figures across history including Socrates, Joan of Arc, Leon Trotsky, and Malcolm X were all quite literally victims of political correctness campaigns, the origins of the contemporary term under discussion here are specific. Having watched the national political picture shift from the promising panoramas of the Kennedy and Johnson victories over Nixon and Goldwater during the early 1960s to an internecine talking-heads quarrel among Republicans and Southern Democrats over the last two decades, many left-leaning Americans opted for a "think globally; act locally" strategy to find a vehicle for personal political expression. Although for activists this may have meant working for regional anti-poverty programs or ecology movements or abortion rights defense, many professional intellectuals, especially those working outside the hard sciences, translated the term "locally" into "rhetorically."

Without an international movement to adhere to, or a nation to govern, or even a party to belong to, politics becomes a pretty bleak activity, especially for thinking people who are born, or who are trained, to imagine human perception as an ideologically generated product. Without cells or churches or even terrorist gangs that attract intellectual energy, America stashes its idealistic and utopian political thinking in universities, occasionally letting it run free a bit during the first few months of a new Democratic party presidency. As long as there isn't too much leakage, no one seems to care much what goes on inside the storage facility.

Lacking vital connections to active centers of power, politically progressive academicians have been forced to imagine positive roles for themselves in a society generally indifferent to their subject matters and downright numb to their ideas. Particularly enraged by the smile button arrogance of the Reagan presidency, many responded by drawing a moral line at the campus gates behind which they could tighten their control over the tiny fiefdoms of their classrooms and department committees, granting favor or exile to those who accepted or rejected their theoretical and linguistic proscriptions. The kingdom of rhetoric was declared a republic and the guillotine made sharp for enemies of the people who might dare to identify themselves. Perhaps the epic games of history were being played in a sandbox, but at least they were being played.

In sitcom terms it was as if Alex Keaton (Michael J. Fox) of *Family Ties* was required to take a course with Mike "Meathead" Stivic (Rob

Reiner) of *All in the Family.* In class one day Professor Meathead is saying something affirmative about affirmative action. Alex straightens his tie and cries, "Quotas!" In a grand conceit of American intellectual and broadcast history Meathead roars, "Stifle yourself!" thus invoking the political legacy of his arch nemesis Archie Bunker. Ironic? Sad? Does this kind of stuff make Walt Whitman weep in eternity? Or has the Great Mandala simply met up with *Wheel of Fortune?* Excuse me for being a TV critic; I now return discourse to more honored channels.

Political correctness, despite the sarcasm it inspires, is not always a bad thing, not by a long shot. The general purging from American polite conversation of such once commonly used words as *nigger, kike, spic, dago, dyke, faggot, gimp,* and oh so many others, can be directly attributed to the fact that these words have become politically incorrect. Ditto for certain usages, such as referring to adult members of particular groups as "girls" and "boys." I am old enough to remember segregationist politicians using the word "nigras" on TV as a diplomatic compromise designed not to offend either those racist members of their constituencies who preferred the word "niggers" *or* any "Negro-lovers" who might be tuning in. I can also remember taking a gym class in junior high school that actually included a lesson on how to not walk like a fag, which I already had a good idea that I was, the peculiarities of my pedestrian style notwithstanding.

This kind of crap hurts people. It creates *others*—subhuman, non-human or parahuman *others*—who can be disregarded, mocked, and even physically brutalized with the special ease reserved for separate species. Social and consequent political pressure has removed dozens of such words and usages from virtually all public discourse (i.e., the mass media). In fact, users of such terms, of whom there remain many, automatically identify themselves as vulgar, ignorant, or at the very least, as outside of the mainstream of public discourse. This was not always so.

But political correctness, as practiced over the last twenty years has matured toward an ominous style of decay. A strange collection of mutant McCarthyites and crackpot culture commissars has taken to scouring the language of others for hints, clues, insinuations, and connotations of racism, sexism, sexual preferentialism, mesomorphilism, and a host of other prejudices to which the unlevel playing field of life can be attributed.[1] Ironically, the failure of society to embrace the principles and practices of universal equality is blamed on a bunch of moral inferiors who must be told they are not fit to converse with civilized people.

One result of these ad hoc investigations of the political morality of those who dare to speak with loose tongues in the fascist-free zones has been the imposition of self-censorship, often by people of good will who do not wish to offend or, of increasing importance, who do not wish to project the appearance that they might wish to offend. It is even fashionable to advertise an idea of just how mortified you are likely to become should you offend. In the case of students taking courses for grades, the worst racists and sexists among them are well aware of what is naughty and what is nice and usually act accordingly when reciting or rewriting for teacher.

A related consequence of this atmospheric engineering has been the turning of college professors into puritanical parents who are ready and willing to publicly punish any and all offenders of the decreed spiritual order. Perhaps the most counterproductive development of all has been the fetishizing of nasty, brutal, and genuinely repulsive language into the elevated status of taboo. In an era when many students need not and do not think twice about using words such as *fuck* and *shit* in classroom discussions, words such as *nigger, chick,* and *fag* may have usurped the functional energy of an eternal adolescent rite. The rising tides on American college campuses of gay-bashing, racial attacks, and rape at the very least prove that political correctness is failing as an educational strategy; at most, there may be some cause-and-effect relationship at work. As Merle Miller wrote in his "coming out" article in *The New York Times Magazine*, "The definition of a faggot is the homosexual gentleman who just left the room."[2]

The most dangerous reactionaries in American society—and here I'm talking about Pat Buchanan and Pat Robertson, not the Klan members who still wear the hoods—make great points with both the voting and the bashing publics by simply focusing attention on the willingness of vigilante language cops to disregard the civil liberties of America's less sensitive souls. The two Pats and their followers, like the corrections officers they criticize, are unabashed and unreluctant censors, and it is not hard to figure out which group is likely to get most of the work should censorship become an expanding industry in America. Let's face it folks, whether you carry an ACLU card or not, freedom of speech means having to bear (if not defend) the right of assholes to say the cruelest, most asinine things possible. Will the successful defense of this principle make America into some kind of Weimar Frankenstein leading its own death charge into fascism? I honestly don't think so. That said, I don't mind admitting that if convinced otherwise, I would renounce everything I've just written. Yes, I'd sooner scold people for calling each other bad names than join *The 700 Club*.

On the Road to Political Correctness: Rodney King and the Video Transfer of History

In the spring of 1992, while working as a paid consultant to an arm of the U.S. government, political correctness got in my face. What can be learned from a quirky anecdote filtered through the prejudiced memory of a predisposed party? Please let me tell you a story. It was a hot April Wednesday afternoon in Los Angeles, the kind of day that might have been a pretty good day, even a beautiful day, except for the pound-and-a-half of hydrocarbons you had to eat every time you drew breath. I cruised La Cienega Boulevard in light traffic to the airport and parked my Brazilian-built VW in the long-term lot. The shuttle bus was dominated by a fair demographic sample of the California flying public: business folk wearing too much clothing for the weather and students wearing not enough clothing for public spaces. I was catching an afternoon flight for D.C. and Uncle Sam was paying the freight.

For the past two months I'd been reading grant proposals for the National Endowment for the Humanities (NEH). Even in that twelfth year of the Reagan-Bush error, the government remained reasonably well-endowed and the NEH should not be confused with its more controversial cousin, the National Endowment for the Arts (NEA). While the NEA was taking heat for showing a lot of naked guys with visible abdominal muscles sitting on each other's faces and sending you-know-who on a deep sea adventure in a barrel of piss, the NEH was going about its kinder, gentler business of funding documentaries that might teach PBS viewers a thing or three about the history of this great, if flawed, nation.

The hot topics among the two dozen or so half-pound grant proposals that had dogged me from deskside since March were these: (1) "race and ethnicity," a phrase used to categorize projects focused on the history and culture of, in alphabetical order, African Americans, Asian Americans, and Native American peoples, these constituting about half the pile; (2) "gender," a term describing the eight or so proposals concerning the lives and times of undervalued heterosexual women who had enough on the ball to keep journals and diaries; and (3) "miscellaneous," the category encompassing all other areas of grant-worthy human interest and experience. Several in this last bunch were about the settling of the American West that year, but, pay those taxes reassured, not a single one of these promoted love, adoration, or sympathy for white men who committed murder or rape, traded smallpox-infested blankets for arable or mineral-rich lands, or thundered across the plains on hostile-looking horses with swords drawn.

So here I was, sitting on an airplane, making a last-ditch attempt at thumbing through one or two of the more incomprehensibly written proposals, on my way to our nation's capital to sit down with a bunch of esteemed colleagues to decide which of this year's crop of desperate independent filmmakers were going to get an injection from Fort Knox to make the movie of her or his dreams, or at least get the rent paid on the loft for the better part of a year, that itself being no mean achievement. While changing planes at Dallas-Fort Worth, I learned from one or more of the many television sets whose signals were bleeding out of the various bars around the terminal (this is perhaps the true meaning of "public television") that the Rodney King verdict had come back in Simi Valley, and that Los Angeles, including some parts close to or even including white neighborhoods, was going up in flames.

It's impossible to go on without stopping here to say a few words about Rodney King, a man who midway through life's journey was remade by and for television. Los Angeles is of course the company town of world TV production and perhaps it is fitting that a videotape, even an extremely independent production such as this, prompted such a profound catastrophe for the city and its residents.

In his 1957 essay, "The White Negro," Norman Mailer wrote that in America "no Negro can saunter down a street with any real certainty that violence will not visit him on his walk."[3] Apparently all that has changed is the level of technology; the victim need no longer be traveling by foot. But the trial of the cops who did the beating in this case was also conducted at a new level of technology. In essence, the courtroom became an arena for a debate that can only be described as an exercise in television criticism. Two TV critics, one the prosecutor, the other the defense attorney, endeavored to interpret a videotape, which served in this case as what the French and their fans like to call *"zee tehhxt."* The prosecutor said, "Well, you've seen the tape so let me tell you what it really meant: these cops mercilessly beat this man beyond all necessity and for no good reason." Undaunted, the defense attorney responded, "O.K., you've seen the tape so let me tell you what it really meant: these cops did their duty in subduing and arresting this dangerous criminal." Instead of twelve hundred Nielsen families, the sample group here consisted of a traditional if somewhat unscientific twelve jurors. O.K. audience, you've seen the show and heard the reviews. Who's got it right, Siskel or Ebert?

And "The Rodney King Beating" was not the only racy "reality program" that had been receiving repeated airplay in Los Angeles during the spring 1992 television season. There was another videotape, this one shot from the automatic ceiling camera of a mom-and-pop grocery store. It featured San Wa Doo, Korean-American immigrant entrepreneur, shooting to death Latasha Harlans, African-American teenager, over the putative theft of a container of orange juice. Here too the court of TV criticism had been convened. The tape played in media loop for months. In court, prosecutor and defense attorney jousted to convince viewers of what they had "really" seen. Once again, both sides failed to call me or any other professional TV critic as an expert witness.

What if instead of buying a hand-held video camera for his new consumer toy that fateful day, plumber George Halliday had bought a "Let's Learn To Paint" set and submitted his rendering of the King incident—in acrylics on canvas—to a local television station, or better yet to the Los Angeles Museum of Contemporary Art? It was only less than two hundred years ago that Napoleon schlepped painters with him across Europe to document his battles. But of course painting has been losing its credibility as a documentary medium since that time. The intensive filtering of event through individual personality makes the process of painting too "subjective" to be trusted any more. Painting requires special talents on the part of the imagemaker; while the camera, as J. Hoberman has written, is "a machine by which any idiot could create a perfect representational likeness."[4] Had the amateur videotape auteur painted an amateur picture of the Rodney King beating instead, it is unlikely that the canvas would have been or could have been offered as evidence of anything in court. Instead, Mr. Halliday would have been compelled to appear and, no matter which medium he felt to be his strongest, he would have been forced to take an oath and testify verbally and probably to sign affidavits as well.

It is only since the invention of the camera that recorded documentation has begun to supersede direct human witness as a legally recognized measure of the past. The search for authentic "objective" records has led some historians to reimagine their work as "social scientific research," rather than as imaginative thinking and writing about the past. I remember as a college freshman signing up for a course on the American Revolution. Despite all my cynicism (this was 1968) something deep inside me actually yearned to be warmed by some flame of freedom that might be flickering behind the facade of the well known petite-bourgeois conflagration of 1776. Even if rages for justice and liberty were nowhere to be found, and the whole kit-and-kaboodle, from the Declaration of Independence and Crispus Attucks to Betsy Ross and Valley Forge, turned out to be just an attempt to dodge taxes and preserve slavery, I was willing to swallow what might be that bitter pill in the name of learning something about just exactly what was what with this mythic land that had drawn my grandparents to drop in from such remote corners of the globe as Bucovina, Romania, and Bialystok, Poland. All four of them had made the trip without ever seeing a single episode of an American television series or a Hollywood movie.

But what did I get for my early-Alfred-Kazin-like idealism in this history course on the American Revolution? A tall, almost willowy graduate student named Mr. Barnes comes strolling into class and announces with a knowing smirk that "History *is not* memorizing a bunch of facts and dates. Anyone can do that. History *is* an attempt to understand documentation so that we might construct a plausible picture of the past." Fair enough, I think, having not the slightest idea of what he is talking about, except for the remark about names and dates, which every history teacher since the seventh grade has made on the first day of class, though you wouldn't necessarily know it from the questions that ended up on the final exam. The subject of Mr. Barnes' next two classes was whether or not Thomas Paine's *Common Sense* was an "authentic document," an issue that I personally thought would have been better resolved before being asked to shell out six bucks for it. I dropped history and added anthropology, where I consumed my share of the cooked and the raw instead.

Perhaps had I stayed in that history course with Mr. Barnes I would have been better prepared to tackle the coming legal and moral questions raised by the general availability of quick, cheap, and ubiquitous documentary technologies, such as tape recorders and videocams. As it is, I can only offer the following meditation on how American historiography made its way from Francis Parkman to *Entertainment Tonight* in a mere two centuries or so. Not surprisingly the key development was the introduction of television:

The American 1950s. An ancient time in an aboriginal place that The History Channel is likely to recall as the Bel Age of Mass Culture. Interstate highways crawl out beyond city limits as urban tax bases crumble before bulldozers. Antennae sprout on rooftops while the first baby tubers plant roots in sofa cushions. Juvenile delinquency enjoys the pre-crack vitality of its own adolescence. Frozen foods defrosting all the day long on formica countertops. Push-down toasters brown fortified white bread. Tuna fish sits placidly in heavy oil. Cars get eight miles per gallon—and we're talking Leaded Super.

At what price, all this? What fool would dare ask? It had not yet become abundantly apparent that everything came complete with cancer and/or a heart attack already inside. Only the period equivalent of shopping cart persons might venture to suggest that earth was anything but real estate to be developed, much less that it was some kind of great nest or, even worse, that it was being sullied. You did not merely smoke on airplanes—the airline gave you the cigarettes for free in convenient promotional three-packs! Consumers strolled with impunity beneath the thinning ozone layer in open-air unenclosed shopping centers at a time when none dared call them malls, "shopping centers" being such an attractive modern term.

With the coming of cable the bold phalluses of ancient communiculture went flaccid on the rooftops. Whereas magnificent towers had democratically cast their signals broadly to any and all, come who may, satellites now circled the planet beaming surgical waves not at vast masses of nameless, faceless citizens, but rather at target markets: at men and at women, at rich and at poor, at 18 to 34 and at 35 to 55 year-olds, at premium channel subscribers and at nonpremium channel subscribers.

Demographia, goddess of North America, queen of all that is plastic, powerful and technodeterministically unavoidable. . . . Demographia, whose holy scriptures are road signs, whose temple is the Super 8 Motel, who stocks the salad bars with plenty and who offers her children All You Can Eat. Movies are your miracles. Radio is your conscience. Television is your oracle; Entertainment Tonight, *our daily vespers.*

In his "Theory of Mass Culture," Dwight Macdonald described the object of the preposition as a "reciprocating engine" in the service of "the Lords of Kitsch."[5] He offered a prediction, paraphrased here with forty years of hindsight: the braintrust of Schlock, Inc., faced with an endless search for more product to fill up the expanding voids of countless new media, would eventually manage to adapt, vulgarize, and over-expose every authentic story, style, and angle of vision that literate High Culture had fastidiously produced over the millennia. And then where would The Industry get its concepts from? With Othello the beneficiary of affirmative action, and Oedipus and Mom appearing on *Geraldo* to tell the story of how they are living, with counseling, happily ever after in a Sunbelt condo, Mass Culture would finally have nothing left to feed off, but itself.

For thousands of years drama and information were scarce. Few people could read and there were few books for those who could. Few plays were produced in few theaters with few seats reserved for a few members of a few social classes. In Darwinian terms, the difficulties facing an idea seeking dissemination were so intense that only the strongest and heartiest among them could survive the rigors of the system; in Hollywood terms, distribution was a bitch.

Electronic mass communication reversed the problem. Distribution becomes a cinch. The trickle of ideas becomes a torrent. The supply of quality resources runs low as the human imagination simply cannot feed the humming engines of production with enough high-grade raw material. The strip-mining of reality begins. The story of Amy Fisher and Joey Buttafuco, once worth perhaps a half a dozen headlines and pictures in the *New York Daily News,* is now worth three made-for-TV movies: a Long Island Lolita for millions who never heard of Vladimir Nabokov, much less ever read him or a satiric novel. (I have encountered students at accredited colleges and universities in the United States today who complain bitterly about being forced to watch black-and-white movies, never mind static black symbols on white paper.)

At dusk each day viewers are offered twin news programs. As the sun goes down, the network anchorpeople make their daily collective journal entry into the Register of Rational Secular Humanist History: bombs and hostages, revolutions and coup d'etats, mergers and acquisitions, a heart-warming story about a surviving artisan in rural North Carolina who still does it the old-fashioned way. But as the moon comes up, *Entertainment Tonight* materializes with the Electric Pagan News of the Day: an exclusive on Zsa Zsa's wardrobe for her assault trial; in-depth interviews with grandchildren of the Three Stooges on the anniversary of Moe's death; a history of racism from Andy Rooney to Jimmy the Greek to Marge Schott. If primitive media critics believed that the News was just so much PR, it can now safely be said with that PR has become just so much of the News.

Time, once calculated in the West by the birth of Christ, is now more thoroughly defined by these two eras: Before Visual Documentation (BVD) and After Visual Documentation (AVD). The BVD period is stored in books and in college courses. It is representationally painted in oil on pre-camera canvasses. It dwells in the soul of the Scholastic Aptitude Tests. Though occasionally referred to on *Jeopardy*, the "before" era is mostly a dark and murky mystery. Imagine coming home . . . and there is no TV to turn on. People once lived that way.

The AVD period, by contrast, is a period of enlightenment. Everything is all too clear. Each year, on the anniversary of the dropping of the first atomic bomb, we take a moment to witness the great mushroom cloud silently blooming over the Pacific Rim horizon on TV. That evening, *Entertainment Tonight* makes its dutiful reports: the week's soap opera ratings, blockbuster movie gross receipts, innovative rock concert riot control techniques, and the entry and discharge log of sick and recovering celebrities at Cedars-Sinai Hospital. In honor of the day's historical significance, a special feature: coverage of the making of a controversial new miniseries, "*Hiroshima,* starring Richard Chamberlain. A Vulgar Sell-Out of a Tragic Event . . . or New Opportunities for Asian-American Actors?"

If prose fiction was an imaginative response to the age-old scarcity of information then it surely lacks that purpose now.[6] The technological marvel of a big fat novel and a public that hungered to learn the events and manners and attitudes inside it is itself the subject for a historical miniseries. The world inhabited by an American mind in the waning moments of the twentieth century is so overloaded with information delivery capacities that the hunt for factoidal infobits—just to fill up the time—has become relentless and exhausting. Faced with this crisis the media conglomerates have gone so far as to recruit the audience to forage the countryside for its own aesthetic sustenance. Examples include *America's Funniest Home Videos, America's Funniest People,* and all public access cable shows. Not only must the audience watch the commercials; it must supply the show. Even the police have been recruited to replace the actors who once portrayed them. In series such as *Cops, True Stories of the Highway Patrol,* and *Rescue 911* real police cars and real police are smashed to bits before the camera, saving expensive stunt overhead. In made-for-TV movies, the studios make use of the viewers' own psychotic episodes to reinvigorate the field of naturalistic narrative that a century of over-harvesting has left in a state of depletion. The daytime talkshows have brought the carnival freak show display to post-Freudian flower.

Pity the poor professor who must compete for attention in this overstimulated bazaar of information. Pity the poor professor who must pump up every intellectual statement with the moral steroids of political correctness to be heard and believed by students who have prepared for class by watching several thousands of hours of TV. But please, don't pity the poor professor enough to allow events such as the one that follows to take place.

Nobody's Fascist

The political correctness anecdote at last: We—the National Endowment for the Humanities 1992 Film and Media Awards Committee—are buzzing along nicely, throwing bricks of taxpayer gold at progressive, educational documentary film, video, and radio projects like so many culture-loving Ignatzes, when we reach a proposal titled "Nobody's Girls," concerning black, Hispanic, and Native American women on the Kansas-Nebraska prairie during the middle to late nineteenth century. The filmmakers have solid records of previous accomplishment. Their project has been endorsed by the requisite experts. Their proposed budget is high enough so that we can be assured that they are professionals, but low enough so that we are unlikely to become easy pickings for right-wing, taxpayer watchdog groups. Their topic is a four-way winner. Let's get on with it; I know how I'm going to vote. And then a dissenting voice.

"I think the project is valid," says a member of the committee, a woman, sexual orientation unknown, holding the chair of a history department at a major American university, "but there is just one thing: the title. I think funding should be contingent upon the changing of the title."

The title? "What's wrong with the title?" I ask with an innocence that I can only describe as prelapsarian.

The historian, a white woman, sexual orientation unknown, acknowledges my question with a pained frown, staring at my name tag for a moment, and sighing as if to say to me, "Oh, come on. What kind of game are you trying to play? *You know* what's wrong with the title. Why are you going to make me spell it out? Are you a right-wing crackpot who's just making believe that he doesn't see the problem, or just looking for some attention?" Remember, she doesn't actually say this to me, but manages to get it all across by means of a single, killer glance.

The thought crosses my mind for a split second that the fact that the word "girl" appears in the title has something to do with it. But the better part of my nature resists the idea that any person possessing the raw intelligence and language skills that must be necessary to be a professor of anything would understand the simple play on words in the title. I am moved to sudden spontaneous, silent prayer, a personal rhetorical stance I usually reserve for totally hysterical moments during which I have no control over circumstances, such as death, tax audits, and job interviews. My entreaty to the Prime Mover? "No, please God, don't let it be the fact that the word 'girl' is in the title."

"We are women," she instructs me, "and we don't like to be referred to as girls."

I suffer for a moment from the paranoid fallacy that this is in fact the Lord's direct rejoinder to my prayer. I achieve balance, however, by recalling that as a confused agnostic, I must always accept the possibility of being alone in a cold, objective universe where order is merely a subjective, wish-based superimposition on objective chaos. In either case prayer is not working, so I turn to reason. "Yes, but don't you see that it's just a play on words. 'Nobody's Girls,' you know, like 'nobody's fool.' It's a kind of pun. You might even say it's a feminist pun at that. These women are 'nobody's girls' and therefore not girls at all."

For my trouble I graduate in her eyes—deep, deep, deep in her eyes —from thick-headed, unhip, and/or a possible political weirdo to stone-cold enemy. She is not embarrassed by not "getting" the joke, though I think, "Damn it, she should be." Instead I'm the one who is supposed to be embarrassed for seeing a joke in such a serious abuse of women and language. She cares not a whit that she is patronizing the artists—female and male—who are making the film and who created and settled on this title.

After several seconds, she makes a verbal response. In a kind of rudimentary whine, in a tone that took me back to the verbal injuries that children inflicted upon one another in the schoolyard of P.S. 180 in Brooklyn, in a primal kvetch that owes something to Androgynous Pat from *Saturday Night Live,* she ejaculates, "You're a man and you just don't understand how much that word hurts."

A dozen scholars with a century of schooling among them sit in paralyzed silence: nobody's fascist.

Such drama! Such action! Such an irrefutable, untoppable demonstration of sensitivity! If I were as sensitive as she thought she was, my peristalsis would have reversed on the spot and the results would have flown in her direction without the benefit of conscious aim. But frankly, I was more dumbfounded than anything else, leaving me at a loss for words. Sensing this, she cruised right along, "And so I really feel we should make funding contingent on a less offensive title. This is a sound project and there's no reason to ruin it with an unfortunate title. After all, as a taxpayer, I don't want my money being spent to

promote something that will injure people—*especially* if it is meant
·as some kind of sick joke," she snarls, casting the last bit of attention
my way.

Would anyone else on the committee support her? That wasn't clear.
All eyes, including mine, were darting randomly around the table, but
still nobody was saying a word, orally or otherwise. At this point, an
official from the Endowment stood up and with the emotionlessness of a
referee at a badminton match who has been asked to explain an obscure
call, he read us the riot act. As an awarding committee we were not
entitled to demand any specific changes in project content, but only
empowered to accept or reject the application as written. The bomb
diffused, we voted unanimously to advise funding of the project. I won-
dered if the chairperson of the history department of a major American
university was counting this as a victory for the forces of reaction. I
know I didn't feel like I was ruler of the world.

So, what's the big deal, you might ask. Political correctness changed
nothing; in fact, it was thwarted. What am I bellyaching about? I don't
mind telling you. First of all, the fact that not one of the dozen women
or men on that committee was willing to speak up against such a profoundly self-aggrandizing and otherwise purposeless display, strikes me
as a very bad case of the emperor's new clothes. Secondly, the utter
humorlessness that prevented the offended party from actually understanding what the producers of "Nobody's Girls" were saying in their
title is chilling, painful, and a bad harbinger for the future of language,
the humanities and humanity. Third on this list, and by no means least
important, is the quickness, the knee-jerk willingness, of madame chairperson to take a censor's blue pencil and make a slash at an artistic
expression that she failed to understand. Remember, a person with this
kind of attitude toward word play, with this kind of sensibility, has read
and critiqued thousands of pages of student writing. That is so depressing, that at the risk of getting a little melodramatic myself, I tell you
the very thought of it just makes me want to die.

And Finally a Word on Cultural Pluralism

If there remains a worthwhile, left-wing position in America that
opposes or at least argues briskly with capitalism as an economic system
and a way of life, it springs from a belief that the common interests of
all people living in a polyglot population are best served by the building
of an integrated society in which citizenship would become synonymous

with humanity and humanity would be valued over all else. Under such logic, religious, ethnic, and racial distinctions would not be recognized by the state as legitimate criteria for special privilege or burden. Neither, it must follow, would gender or sexual preference. Was this ever true in the past? No. Is such a meritocracy possible? Hard to say. Is it worth fighting for or at the very least supporting rhetorically? Yes.

For eighty years or so many people who became or called themselves Communists or Socialists or Progressives did so because of beliefs in these principles. During and since the 1960s, however, the precipitates of such elevated thinking plopped to earth as Leonid Brezhnev playing a game of "Let's Blow Up the World" with the Pentagon, François Mitterand bringing a fresh management style to French capitalism, and a professor of history at a major American university deeming a coy pun as an unacceptable political crime. Why did this happen? Perhaps human beings are not good enough as a species to support the institutionalization of fairness on anything close to a mass level.

In America, which hasn't had a publicly engaged left wing beyond the margin of the Democratic party since it was successfully amputated during the early 1950s by the McCarthyites, we must return to the playpen of the university to discover the fate of Marxism as it detaches itself from Russian apparatchiks and French intellectuals and floats off into the post-modern effluvia. What we find is not a pretty sight. There is, of course, the straight-faced acting out of infantile fantasies, as in the case of nobody's girl. But intra-Beltway incidents such as these are distant from the day-to-day operations of contemporary education. The meat and potatoes of political correctness can be found on the mimeographed pages of course syllabi and in the debates over the curricula that shape them. Whereas once (i.e., in the 1960s) opposition to required reading lists and required courses was itself a left-wing position, now the self-annointed heirs to post-Communist Marxism have become the advocates of a whole new set of academic requirements.

Cultural pluralism is a broad educational agenda, that has usurped the ideological position once held by the "melting pot" metaphor, which until the 1960s was promoted as a basic article of American faith. Originally Emerson's "smelting pot" of metal alloys, the metaphor was transformed in general use to a culinary image. It is a vision of American culture as a single bubbling stew whose taste is the sum of the contributions of its diverse ingredients. Though now largely discredited as a reactionary cover-up for the imperial rule of northwestern Eurocentrism, the melting pot must have seemed quite progressive at one time, especially in the face of the various waves of white supremacism, know-nothingism, and other forms of recurring racist nativism that it challenged.

For better or for worse, a melting pot or anything like it was never achieved and perhaps it never could have been. But several factors did the melting pot in among the cultural cognoscenti while it was still nothing more than a germinating idea. The post-World War II civil rights movement, whose fundamental commitment to destroy Jim Crow had made it an offspring of melting-pot ideology, shifted its focus away from the idealization of integration during the 1960s and 1970s and toward the cultivation of black identity, which in many cases meant black separatism. The assassination of Martin Luther King, Jr., was an historical marker in this regard. King had always promoted a goal of black assimilation into a mainstream (real or imagined) of American life. King's death seemed to leave melting-potism at a cul-de-sac. For some members of minority groups, assimilation, the abstract idea to which the melting pot metaphor refers, has since evolved into something of a negative buzz word. The Nation of Islam, the Jewish Defense League, and the Aryan People's Nation can all agree on this.

Also after World War II, and perhaps of equal impact concerning the disintegration of the melting pot metaphor among the educated and educators, millions of white middle-class families, borrowing money from solvent S & L's, fled ethnically marked urban neighborhoods for the great promised land of the melting pot faithful: the suburban tract development. Much to their dismay, however, these depression-born moms and dads saw many of the best and brightest of their children grow up to resent the sterile homogeneity of winding lane life. The melting pot, once touted for its spiciness, had yielded a rather bland broth to the taste of a significant element of the new bourgeoisie that emerged from the Vietnam era. These self-defined creatures of taste, these lickers of imported ice cream cones, grinders of exotic coffee beans, and sippers of water flowing from anywhere but a tap, preferred a pinch of funky organic root to another tablespoon of Levittown MSG. It is from this group of tasty post-war suburban children that disproportionate numbers of American college professors sprang as the higher education industry boomed out of all historical proportion.

And so in the last two decades the melting pot seems to have gone the way of the blue plate special and the ink well. Its replacement in educational mythology, cultural pluralism, is an ideal that recognizes and celebrates the continuing survival of pre-American and para-American identities. The cultural pluralist prefers to see the nation as the sum of persisting ethnic and racial cultures, rather than as some single entity wrought from various contributions that have melted down in the process. Strangely juxtaposed rhythms may become cacophonous at times, but to the discerning ear of the cultural pluralist anything is preferable to artificially imposed harmony.

The positive results of cultural pluralism are undeniable. Behind the sparkling glitziana of free-market vanilla popcult, dozens of commercially marginal minority literatures, visual arts movements, and performance troupes flourish. The table scraps of the bloated homogeneous mass culture fast food feast sustain poets and videotape-makers in the form of government and foundation grants and public and private teaching positions. If the serious artist wishes to bite the hand that feeds her or him, that hand has thus far been so fleshy so as to only feel a tickle. Freedom of speech goes out on a blind date with the tax write-off and, except for Jesse Helms and some other would-be chaperones, everybody's happy.

But the down side of cultural pluralism mirrors that of political correctness in general. The quality of substance somehow gets buried under the quantification of gesture. The very kind of oversimplification that allows television networks to present "racially balanced" commercials and compels political parties to present "ethnically balanced" tickets has been taken to heart by the political corrections department as a model for the study of the arts. Personal taste, as an individual synthesis of values, intellect, and visceral appreciation, is thus reduced to (I know some would argue, "exposed as") a raw political decision.

One stunning misuse of the pluralist impulse—a stunning misuse that has misused me—has been a willingness to impose cultural quotas on college reading lists. To listen to the current arguments about "required books" you would think that reading Ernest Hemingway somehow becomes an implicit rejection of Richard Wright (and all the demographic baggage he schlepps) or vice-versa. If Hemingway and Wright both manage to appear on the syllabus, who must then be presumed missing? And which one of those two should she be replacing? The anxiety to make sure that students are exposed to this or that *type* of authorial voice in a world where there is an ever-diminishing amount of time and inclination to read books is perhaps understandable. But novels and poems and plays cannot be casually recontextualized into mere tokens or exemplars of collective blood-based or affinity-based cultural enterprises if literature or any of the arts are to be allowed their impacts on people.

The big stink over which authors shall and shall not appear on required reading lists is actually emanating from the rotting foundation of reading time. Highly educated people, like everybody else, are offered an increasing array of information sources these days and books are consistent losers in the competition, whether or not they ought to be. Hardly anybody can bear to get through the *Cliff Notes* anymore. With the number of actual pages read plummeting, the urge to make sure that some of these pages were written by this kind of hand or that becomes an ever more intense political battle.

Yet to put an author in the position of representing a race, a gender, or a set of sexual behaviors is a reductive redefinition of the function of literature that is unfair to medium and genre as well as to writer and reader. There is as much chance in this kind of reading of pinning the flaws of the individual writer on the group that he or she supposedly represents as there is in creating empathy or identity with that group. If the reader dislikes the writing or is bored by it, no amount of fancy critical footwork on the part of a teacher is likely to cover that up.

What is to be done about required reading lists? Frankly, I remain an unreconstructed 1968 college freshman on this subject. Abolish them all. Strive for a faculty philosophically eclectic enough to offer a multiplicity of educational experiences and then start praying that the students read anything at all, which is the real problem and which has thus far proved much too painful and difficult for anyone to deal with.

The whole political correctness thing—from language censorship, to reading list censorship, to the censorship of erotic materials, be they art, pornography, or pornographic art—is a disgrace. The self-imagined radicals who want to wash out their students' and colleagues' mouths with soap have no right to do so. The liberals who are cowed by fear of being thought of as thinkers of bad thoughts ought to be cowed instead by fear of eroding the protections of the Bill of Rights. The conservatives who want to use political correctness to discredit every movement toward racial and sexual equality as some kind of smokescreen for creeping left-wing totalitarianism should instead go to the house of worship of their choice and beg God's forgiveness for selling out the economic future of America in return for short term capital gains. And that means you, Dinesh D'Souza and all the spoiled brat would-be or wannabee rednecks who put out the *Dartmouth Review*.

---

1. Mesomorphilism is the granting of special favor, privilege or status to mesomorphs, people with muscular bodies. In the pecking order of American morphology, ectomorphs (the skinny) finish second with endomorphs (the fat) finishing a distant third.

2. Merle Miller, "What It Means to Be a Homosexual," *New York Times Magazine* 17 Jan. 1971, 9.

3. Norman Mailer, "The White Negro," in *Advertisements for Myself* (New York: Perigree, 1976), 302.

4. J. Hoberman, "Love and Death in the American Supermarketplace," in *Vulgar Modernism* (Philadelphia: Temple Univ. Press, 1992), 46.

5. Dwight Macdonald, "A Theory of Mass Culture," in *Mass Culture: The Popular Arts in America*, ed. B. Rosenberg and D. M. White, (NY: Free Press, 1957), 69.

6. Perhaps this is the reason why minority fictions—especially black and gay or lesbian—are showing such vitality in the United States. Minority cultures that are relatively ignored by network TV and mainstream movies still have practical functional roles for the novel and other literary forms to play.

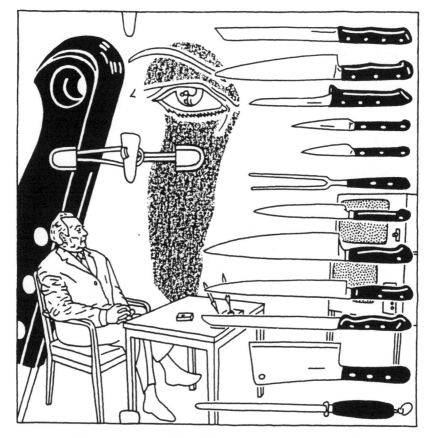

"The best minds of Allen Ginsberg's generation were still
'accusing the radio of hypnotism' in 1955 . . ."

The Emergence of Television Criticism
1920 to 1988

Europe called for Dada by antithesis: America for analogous
reasons called for the antithesis of Dada. For America is Dada.
The richest mess of these bean-spillers of Italy, Germany and
France is a flat accord beside the American chaos. Dada spans
Brooklyn Bridge; it spins round Columbus Circle; it struts
with the Ku-Klux Klan; it mixes with all brands of bootleg
whisky; it prances in our shows; it preaches in our churches;
it tremolos at our political conventions.

—Waldo Frank,
"Seriousness and Dada," 1924

Getting away from the grim words 'mass media,' finding a
new name for them, connecting their social effects with the
pleasures they give—was for me an act of simple justice.

—Gilbert Seldes,
"Preface," *The Seven Lively Arts*, 1957

The uniformity of response from the artistic and intellectual communities
to the introduction of national television service in the United States
following the Second World War is striking. Any enthusiasm for the
democratizing possibilities of the medium or for its homegrown proces-
sional Whitmanian aesthetic was quickly dispelled by a patronizing
glance at the content of the actual programming presented by the three
midtown Manhattan corporate giants who held the keys to the hardware
store: the spectacle of Milton Berle behind falsies vamping in drag while
making homophobic jokes; the ominous monosyllabic police-state dia-
tribes of Jack Webb; the screaming winners of washing machines and
trips to Florida; the brainless oh-goshisms of suburban domestic repre-

sentational comedies; the hollow seductive smiles of the comedy-variety choruslines flirting their way through sexless antidance choreographies.

Given the overpoweringly mass-cult ambience of the new medium, even high-tone series such as Edward R. Murrow's *See It Now* (1952–1955) and Alistair Cooke's *Omnibus* (1953–1957)—programs that during the formative years of the system served a function that has since fallen to the entire PBS network—suffered a kind of guilt by association for being TV shows in the first place. Early television at its selfconscious "best"—the live, commercially segmented, psycho-babbling sub-tragic dramas of Paddy Chayefsky, Rod Serling, and Reginald Rose—was deemed a mere flirtation with midcultery. Ironically it was NBC boss Robert Sarnoff who summed up the "Golden Age of TV Drama" most frankly. In 1961, having concluded that television's dramatic piles of money would be made from filmed shoot 'em ups and car crashes rather than live, dialogue-oriented plays, Sarnoff dismissed the Golden Age his company had helped to create as an overrated exercise in "phoney social philosophy in plays about beatniks and characters full of self-pity."[1] It was not until twenty years after the death of the "playhouse" genre that kinescopes of "Marty," "Requiem for a Heavyweight," "Bus to Nowhere," and other such quasi-modernist efforts were canonized for middle-class adoration as PBS reruns.[2]

If good TV could do no better than wax mediocre, bad TV waned downright descendental. The tube at its unselfconscious "worst"—the whirling checkered coat of Pinky Lee, the resurrection of the Three Stooges from the graveyard of Depression-era Saturday afternoons at the movies, game shows hosted by Bert Parks—was apparently several rings deeper than Man Thinking cared to venture. Marxists, liberals, and beatniks stood shoulder to shoulder with genteel elitists, fundamentalist ministers, and neighborhood librarians in turning a blind eye toward a cultural delivery system that promised to make "the masses" and "the audience" synonymous terms.[3] The best minds of Allen Ginsberg's generation were still "accusing the radio of hypnotism" in 1955; television is mentioned not even once among the stunning catalogue of cultural terrors to be found in "Howl." That very same year, Rodney-Young Productions was proclaiming *"Ars pro multis"* at the end of each new *Father Knows Best* episode. For the masses? Certainly. But where was the art?

Dwight Macdonald and Herbert Marcuse were leading critical figures on the left. For them and other progressives, television was a hopelessly vertical system of cultural distribution, more than willing and only too able to program the responses of the millions to whatever political or consumerist suggestions served the short-term interests of ruthless, relentless capital. The consciousness of the many—the very force that might reform and improve society—was shamelessly squandered on self-destructive romantic fantasies at the expense of participatory urge and collective vision. Marcuse warns the reader against dangerous "new forms of control." The apparatus of mass communications, in Marcuse's view, creates a "closed language (which) does not demonstrate and explain—it communicates decision, dictum, command."[4]

In his 1956 essay, "The Phantom World of TV," Gunther Anders modeled socialist response to television when he wrote, "Modern mass consumption is a sum of solo performances; each consumer, an unpaid homeworker employed in the production of mass man."[5] The viewer is seen as a pathetic stooge (and we're talking Larry here, not even Curly) performing a cultural tragedy whose terrifying implications are far more aesthetically compelling than the low slapstick gestures of a Ball, a Gleason, or a Skelton. In his 1957 film *A Face in the Crowd*, Elia Kazan speaks to the concerns of educated mainstream liberalism when he warns the American public that television could destroy the integrity of the electoral system by thrusting political power into the kissers of opportunistic actors and spokespersons and their right-wing handlers. Nah . . .

Questions of authorship, genre, and discourse were almost completely ignored in post-war mass media studies. Indeed specific television programs are not even mentioned in such seminal television-era works as Macdonald's "A Theory of Mass Culture" or Marcuse's *One-Dimensional Man*. Described only in terms of its systemic effects, TV is seen as a kind of relentlessly ringing bell in a vast Pavlovian laboratory of culture. If the tongues salivate whether or not a stimulus is offered, why discuss the flavor or quality of the dogfood? *I Love Lucy?* Fascism with a laughtrack.

On the Right, conservatives such as T. S. Eliot, R. P. Blackmur, and Ernest van den Haag feared the intrusion of commercialization on the personal spheres of family, religion, and *volk*. As was the case with their left-leaning counterparts, these commentators rarely mention the word "television," much less any program titles. Perhaps it was the apparently increasing dependence upon TV of capitalism itself that provoked this caution on the part of conservatives. In his "Notes Toward the Definition of Culture" (1949), Eliot already fears the Americanization of Britain as the first television licenses are issued in his adopted homeland. The Missouri-born poet identifies religion as the structural human impulse that makes the development of all culture possible.[6] Without tribal or national consensus on the etiology of the universe, standards of good and evil inevitably deteriorate into relativity. Lacking a clear moral foundation, art becomes pornography: gratuitous titillation leading to chaotic disruption of order and community.

America's pluralism had been its aesthetic albatross in the minds of reactionaries since long before the excesses of the twentieth century had sent the likes of T. S. Eliot and Ezra Pound fleeing across the Atlantic toward Byzantium. European cultural conservatives from Count de Tocqueville to José Ortega y Gasset had been similarly repulsed by what Whitman, even before the Civil War, was celebrating as a "teeming nation of nations."[7] Television, a medium structurally compromised to serve a maximum number of segments of an already mongrelized society, was the nightmarish precipitate of the American experiment to the aesthetically cleansed sensibility. The self-appointed keepers of the castle, charged with the eternal care of the best that has been thought and said, fretted beneath the intimidation of a cultural bomb whose fall-out threatened the survival of the entire aesthetic ecos. *I Love Lucy?* Stalinism with a laughtrack.

The current of books and essays that greeted the introduction of broadcasting into American culture has since been labeled by intellectual historians as "The Mass Culture Debate." It was not, however, much of a debate. Socialist as well as conservative participants found too much common ground in their shared vocational identities. For example, in 1953 Dwight Macdonald complained of the blandness and emptiness of mass culture. He accused the great leisure-industry corporations of homogenizing the best of both high culture and folk culture in their never-ending quest for broadly marketable products. Mass culture, wrote Macdonald, "threatens to engulf everything in its spreading ooze."[8] The similarity of conservative thinking on this issue is obvious in the following passage from *The Fabric of Society,* a collaborative work by Michael Ross and Ernest van den Haag:

> The mass media inexorably exclude art and anything of significance when it cannot be reduced to mass entertainment, but (instead) they divert us from the passage of the time they keep us from filling. They tend to draw into the mass market talents and works that might otherwise produce new visions, and they abstract much of the capacity to experience art or life directly and deeply.[9]

As intellectuals, all feared the threat of a total corporate takeover of culture; as professional book writers, all dreaded the consequences of the outmoding of their craft. "Us" was *Kultur* (from the Bible to Picasso); "them" was television (from Madison Avenue to Hollywood).

Several liberal critics, such as David Manning White and Melvin Tumin could even go so far as to allow that tolerating the brainless screech of television—leaking through the walls from a neighbor's set—was the aesthetic price that would have to be paid by artists and intellectuals for the privilege of living in non-totalitarian states in the twentieth century.[10] But if there were disagreements at all motivating the "Mass Culture Debate," they were not about whether television was good or bad, worthwhile or worthless, or even structurally capable or incapable of ever improving. In each case, the latter was generally assumed as a ground rule for the serious critic. It seems to me that the real debate was about a question nobody was brave enough to ask aloud: Can we get rid of this TV thing without setting up concentration camps? The answer turned out to be a resounding "No!"

If sales figures and Nielsen ratings meant anything, the public had frankly gone bananas about this household appliance that had conjured the messianic hostility of so many intellectuals. Perhaps television was receiving no worse treatment than had the American cinema fifty years previously. Robert Sklar argues that during the early development of the film industry many of the traditional gatekeepers of American culture— professors and clergymen prominently—resented the way in which they were being circumvented by a bunch of upstart entrepreneurs, many of whom were neither educated nor churched, many of whom were not even native-born.[11] Television, to an even greater degree than the nickelodeon, was loud, vulgar, insufficiently deferential to traditional sensibility, and hopelessly tied up with trade (this last trait as distasteful to Tories as it was insidious to anticapitalist revolutionaries).

Anyone who doubted the dangers of such an instrument to a free society was referred to T. W. Adorno, Walter Benjamin, Erich Fromm, Max Horkheimer, Leo Lowenthal, and the other Frankfurt School theorists who had located the success of Nazi totalitarianism in that party's innovative uses of mass communications technology. With the ink on the Nuremburg verdicts hardly dry, the American TV networks were suddenly using an even more advanced form of high tech masscom to sell toothpaste and Chevrolets. Might they not just as efficiently sell military expansionism or racial genocide, should the political trade winds shift?[12]

It is perhaps not surprising that many German-Jewish refugee college professors seemed to think so. A Luddite urge to wipe away the machine lay just beneath the surface of this fatalistic analysis. Brain workers showed themselves no less fearful of the latter stages of industrialism than brawn workers had shown themselves to be of previous stages. As a result, the question of contention that dominated media criticism as the TV networks were coming to form was this: Is it possible for intellectuals (i.e., the partisans of print) to save culture from television? The optimists said yes; the pessimists said no.

It is of course doubtful that the close reading of television texts by academic or journalistic critics during the 1950s would have had much of an effect on the upbringing of the *enfant terrible*. In *Fifties Television: The Industry and its Critics*, (1993), William Boddy describes, in morbid detail, the institutional immunity that the TV industry built up to aesthetically based criticism after a brief flirtation with it in the medium's infancy.[13] But the upturned noses on the Right and the wringing hands on the Left amounted to an effective disengagement of critical thought from what rapidly became the nation's most important source of drama, news, style, and language. This collective act of rejection by the intellectual community certainly did not hamper the rapid expansion of the medium or of the satellite industries that grew out of its technological advantages. All nightmares came true: television became both the vital engine of consumerist capitalism and the intrusive disrupter of traditional community and family values.

Against this general background, three names stand out as dissenting progenitors of what would survive to the present as a usable critical past: Erik Barnouw, the only historian at work during the 1950s who seemed to grasp the significance of the entertainment-industrial complex as it was being put into place; Marshall McLuhan, the cultural philosopher who attempted to make sense of the new epistemological order of the television age by searching for its contexts in the archives of Western civilization; and Gilbert Seldes, the only critic of note (as opposed to reviewer; no mass circulation newspaper lacked one of those) who dared to offer thick readings of television programs at a time when such material was generally considered beneath the contempt of educated people.

The heirs of these three pioneers became apparent during the 1970s and 1980s. Owing much to Barnouw's efforts, the history of American broadcasting has recently become a flourishing academic subdiscipline. Barnouw's masterwork—his monumental three volume *History of Broadcasting in the United States*—no longer constitutes the entire bibliography on the historical formation of the industry. Its encyclopedic scope, however, has made it a primary reference text for a new generation of American historians whose efforts have gone, as one might expect, to particulars: in *Inventing American Broadcasting 1899–1922*, Susan J. Douglas focuses on the precommercial radio period; in *Media and the American Mind: From Morse to McLuhan*, Daniel J. Czitrom uncovers the response of American intellectuals such as William James,

John Dewey, and Robert Park to the various stages of media development that took place during their lifetimes; J. Fred Macdonald has written issue-oriented historical concordances to entire television programming eras and genres;[14] George Lipsitz has studied the presentation of class and ethnic stereotypes during the 1950s;[15] Thomas Cripps has examined the context of the television adaptation of *Amos 'n' Andy* in the civil rights struggle;[16] and so on. As broadcast history moves toward a second century, the selection of definable periods and topics increases geometrically. William Boddy focuses on the 1950s in *Fifties Television*. Mary Ann Watson takes on the early 1960s in *The Expanding Vista*.

As for McLuhan, he has been a more difficult act to follow. With historically based critical studies of literature and culture in precipitous decline in recent years—with the epistemological value of the humanities itself placed in doubt by orthodox number crunchers and their unwitting deconstructionist allies—few commentators have been willing or able to follow the path of inquiry suggested by *Understanding Media* and *The Gutenberg Galaxy*. An Anglo-Catholic literature professor educated at the University of Manitoba and Cambridge University, McLuhan insisted that the continuities bridging the pre-and post-broadcasting eras were the keys to understanding the disjunctions separating them.

Most English Departments frankly begged to differ, preferring to treat television as if it were not a momentous occasion in the development of the language. The general failure of McLuhan's litcrit Brahmin colleagues to embrace his subject matter has been a disappointment to those who imagine the study of books as a service to the broader studies of language and culture. Moreover, this failure has been a strategic blow to the already shell-shocked humanities, helping to marginalize the aesthetic apprehension of consciousness even further from the centers of public rhetoric.

If literature critics for the most part rejected McLuhan's mandate for the study of the mass media, the social scientists who came to thoroughly embrace McLuhan's subject matter were largely indifferent to his methodology. Having created a profitable industry for themselves by quantitatively proving and disproving the "effects" of television on "the masses" (especially violence and sex), these sociologists and mass psychologists have found little of use in McLuhan's dense, allusion-laden metaphysical *divining*. In an era in which the protestation of empiricism shields the analyst from the stigma of having offered a personal opinion, a freshly laundered lab coat is more comfortable working attire than a dark medieval cowl.

Most specialists with degrees from American universities in subjects such as "communication theory" and "marketing" seem to know or care little about the processes of premechanical bookmaking or the poetry of Alexander Pope (to name just two of McLuhan's "eccentric" entrances into modern media studies). Several literary artists, however, have produced works that have upheld McLuhan's humanistic approach. These include Umberto Eco's *Travels in Hyper Reality* (1983); any of the critical studies of Jacques Ellul, especially *La Technique;* and *White Noise,* the 1984 novel by Don DeLillo (see segment 2). The only American on the list, DeLillo offers a particularly dramatic narrative exploration of "industrial folklore" as suggested by McLuhan's *The Mechanical Bride.*

By contrast, the few direct efforts by American humanities scholars at McLuhanesque broadstroke technocultural critical writing have been pretty dismal. Typically more interested in iterating their own gentility than in examining the subject at hand, these efforts amount to endless recapitulations of the "plug-in drug" arguments. Books by Neil Postman and Gary Gumpert, for example, have embraced McLuhanite *koans* such as "the medium is the message," and "the post-Gutenberg era." But unwilling or unable to effect McLuhan's cool, clinical empire tone, these writers take the easy way out of mass media studies, cautioning the good reader to "just say no" to the "plug-in drug."

Postman's clumsily written *Amusing Ourselves to Death* (1985) epitomizes this romantic regression from the media world. Citing such authorities as "the great Socrates" and "the wise Solomon" (this is actual language appearing in the text), the book is a comprehensive summary of the vast range of schoolmarm objections to television. Its single departure from the "Mass Culture Debate" model of scholarly gentility is Postman's insistence on conjuring nineteenth-century America (rather than eighteenth-century Europe) as the pre-electronic golden age that proves the evil of our current condition.

All of which brings us to Gilbert Seldes. Not nearly as famous as McLuhan or as widely read as Barnouw, Seldes does not even rate an entry in *The New York Times Encyclopedia of Television.* Nor does his name appear in the indexes of such comprehensive textbook histories of American broadcasting as Sterling and Kitross's *Stay Tuned* (1978) or Barnouw's *Tube of Plenty* (1975). Despite this neglect Seldes must be counted as the founder of the critical vocation practiced today by a host of academic and free-lance television critics, including Horace Newcomb, Robert C. Allen, David Thorburn, Patricia Mellencamp, Michael Arlen, Ella Taylor, Thomas Schatz, Caren Deming, Thomas Zynda, Mimi White, Robert Thompson, Jimmie L. Reeves, and Jane Feuer.

Working without VCR, TV reference books, a word processor, or even a taste for gossip, Seldes watched television—and took seriously the task of writing about what he saw—from the moment the invention appeared in the laboratory, publishing a piece titled "The 'Errors' of Television" as early as 1937![17] His remarkable volume of practical criticism, *The Public Arts* (1956), contains specific chapters concerning the performance art of such television stars as Milton Berle, Jack Benny, and Sid Caesar, as well as meditations on a variety of complex issues, including the relationships between cinema and video, and the dominance of comedy over tragedy on prime-time schedules.

The younger brother of the muckraking journalist George Henry Seldes, Gilbert Vivian Seldes was born in Alliance, New Jersey in 1893. Completing a degree at Harvard in 1914, he served as a war correspondent for the *Philadelphia Evening Ledger* before returning to America as Washington correspondent for *L'Echo de Paris*. The Seldes brothers were deeply interested in politics and, like their socialist utopian parents, they counted themselves as advocates—as well as progressive reformers —of American democracy. George would pursue this political passion as a kind of meta-journalist, becoming a print-media watchdog whose work would serve as an example for I. F. Stone and others. Gilbert pursued similar aims in his exploration of the role of popular culture in democracy, adhering to the Whitmanian principle that the measure of democracy's success as a political system would lay in the quality of the popular culture produced under its rule.[18] This belief took him first to the theater, then to the movies, to radio, and finally to television. His willingness to shift critical focus from one medium to the next in response to the evolution of mass communications technology demonstrates a concern in his values for the social and political consequences of art that prevails over the inevitable critical temptation to fetishize medium, genre, or object.

After the end of the First World War, the character of Gilbert Seldes' career quickly took shape. In 1920, he began a four-year stint as managing editor at *The Dial*. The magazine, which had been founded as a cultural monthly in 1880, had only recently abandoned the traditionalist Victorian editorial policies that could be traced to its origins. A new editor, Scofield Thayer, moved *The Dial*'s offices from Chicago to New York, attempting to put it at the crossroads of the radical literary and artistic movements that were reviving following the Armistice. The monthly became a fortnightly and it was rapidly transformed from a nineteenth-century parlor-room review to a self-consciously free-thinking champion of previously taboo culture in America. Randolph Bourne, Van Wyck Brooks, and H. E. Stearns were among Seldes' colleagues on the editorial staff. All of these critics were advocates of what is sometimes described as the "green tradition" in American letters. Identifying strongly with Emerson in theory and Whitman in practice, they were bound by a common conviction that the home-grown in American literature, art, and culture was not to be measured by, or sacrificed to, the preservation of traditional European forms and standards.[19]

At *The Dial*, Seldes handled avant-garde manuscripts by such writers as Thorstein Veblen, John Dewey, and Mary Ritter Beard. He left his editorial position in 1923, but remained *The Dial*'s drama critic until the end of the decade. In his 1924 book, *The Seven Lively Arts*, Seldes proclaimed the reasons for his critical dedication to such "low" popular forms as comic strips, motion pictures, vaudeville, and pop music:

> Because, in the first place, the lively arts have never had criticism. The box-office is gross; it detects no errors, nor does it sufficiently encourage improvement. . . . The lively arts can bear the same continuous criticism we give to the major, and if the criticism itself isn't bogus there is no reason why these arts should become self-conscious in any pejorative sense. In the second place, the lively arts which require little intellectual effort will more rapidly destroy the bogus than the major arts ever can. The close intimacy between high seriousness and high levity, the thing that brings together the extremes touching at the points of honesty and simplicity and intensity—will act like the convergence of armies to squeeze out the bogus. And the moment we recognize in the lively arts our actual form of expression, we will derive from them the same satisfaction which people have always derived from art which was relevant to their existence.[20]

Seldes' personal eclecticism never flagged. The author of several murder mysteries (under the pseudonym Foster Johns), an editor of the works of Ring Lardner, a daily columnist for *The New York Journal*, and an Ivy League professor, he continued to scale the peaks and valleys of American letters for half a century. During the Depression year of 1930, for example, he completed a contemporary stage adaptation of Aristophanes' *Lysistrata* and also wrote a book on the evolving etiquette of social drinking during the Prohibition era. During the 1950s, he was—at the same time—dean of the Annenberg School of Communications at the University of Pennsylvania *and* a weekly series reviewer for *TV Guide* who specialized in sitcoms.

Just as George Seldes' belief in the crucial function played by journalism in American democracy had made him a press critic, Gilbert Seldes' similar belief about the role of drama in a democratic culture put him in front of a television set. It surely took a certain amount of confidence in the years immediately following World War II for an intellectual to devote his career to the aesthetic examination of a medium that was establishing a reputation, almost from birth, as the crudest public exercise of the imaginative capacity in the history of artistic expression. Seldes' impeccable credentials—his family, education, apprenticeship, and early career—must have provided him with some of this confidence. The contingency that he could move freely from academic appointment to commercial writing must have also been a factor.

Seldes' critical embrace of what so many of his colleagues were willing to dismiss as just so much evidence of the sociopathic dysfunction of late capitalism was neither self-serving nor a patronization. In 1956, for example, the critic found himself thoughtfully perplexed by the rise of Jackie Gleason: "throwing his weight around . . . is . . . Gleason's most characteristic movement before the camera. He is a heavy man with the traditional belief of heavy men in their own lightness and grace."[21] Seldes admired Gleason's technical acumen as a comedian, but on the whole, found The Great One "distasteful." The very ambiguity of such comment concerning a leading television performer went against the tide of bland daily "like it or don't like it" newspaper reviewing. But what is far more remarkable about the Seldes critique of Gleason is the fact that a critic with Seldes' training finds fault with the "fatman" TV clown not by way of some comparison with Falstaff or even with Fatty Arbuckle, but rather rates Gleason against the standard of Jimmy Durante, who was hosting a comedy-variety show during the mid-1950s that was much like Gleason's.[22] Seldes found Durante's grotesque mugging and posturing and his stylized Brooklyn speech supported by a humane warmth that he felt was lacking in the blustery tirades of Ralph Kramden or in the egocentric pomposity of Reginald Van Gleason III. Seldes was perhaps the first critic who could discuss matters of taste in television viewing without questioning a taste for television viewing itself.

Seldes refused to isolate television narrative from the traditional paradigms of American culture. A good example of this is his positive review of Paul Henning's *The Beverly Hillbillies,* which was published in *TV Guide* following the sitcom's premiere in the fall of 1962. Unwilling to issue a blanket dismissal of situation comedy in general or rural situation comedy in particular (as most reviewers did in response to what would become the most popular show on American TV during the 1960s), Seldes affords the text the respect of careful viewing and searches for its context:

> The thumping success of *The Beverly Hillbillies* has already sent some serious thinkers to the wailing wall, and when you tune the program in, you are supposed to ask yourself, "What is America coming to?" As I

am still laughing, I think back to the days when custard pies and Keystone Cops were flying through the air and a lot of people were convinced America was a cultural "desert"—the 1920 word for "wasteland." A question I asked then has never been answered: What can you do with a custard pie except throw it?[23]

Thus Seldes stands alone as both a learned and a sympathetic television critic during the first two decades of network broadcast. Unfortunately, that very loneliness led to obscurity rather than distinction. His writing simply did not fit into the high-cult and mass-cult publishing apartheid that was the substance and legacy of "The Mass Culture Debate." Simultaneously more complex than the bubble-gum reviewing of the tabloid TV sections and too simplistic (as much for its lack of disciplinary jargon as for its subject matter) to be taken seriously as academic criticism, the body of Seldes' work simply fell through the cracks in American letters.

Seldes seemed very much aware of this. In his last book, *The New Mass Media: Challenge to a Free Society* (1968), he attempts a metacritical overview of American television, focusing on the philosophical implications of the mass media for American democratic traditions. Abandoning practical criticism completely, the short, pamphlet-like book takes on the character of a Mass Culture Debate tome. Completely out of character for Seldes, it does not mention the name of even a single performer or program in its hundred pages. Although this attempt at a "respectable" treatise is evidence of Seldes' frustration, the critic ends on a hopeful note in the final chapter, reiterating the essence of his lifelong work:

> In many colleges, courses in the communications arts have been established in the past ten years, and in some of these the habit of observing popular entertainment critically is instilled. The new effort is to give students an intelligent outlook on the mass media, not to make them experts in either the aesthetic or the sociological aspects, but to inform their judgment, to make them more selective in their own choices. Such courses may ultimately increase manyfold the number of people who will not apathetically accept whatever is offered. . . . Our schools and colleges would (thus) "create an audience" of thoughtful people so large that they would become a factor in the plans of the entertainment media."[24]

Seldes' idealistic commitment to the basic didactic function of the critical vocation in a democratic culture had survived in him since his days at *The Dial*. It was not, however, until after his death in 1970 that evidence began to arise that his faith was neither misplaced nor was it the merely quaint residue of another age.

The publication of Horace Newcomb's *TV: The Most Popular Art* in 1974 was a watershed for television criticism of the type that Seldes had suggested and advocated. A professor of American Studies holding a doctorate in literature, Newcomb had also worked as a daily television reviewer for *The Baltimore Sun*. He had written a book of criticism on popular commercial TV programs organized as a series of genre studies: the domestic sitcom, the afternoon soap opera, the action-adventure show, and so on.[25] Dependent upon neither statistics nor stimulus-response theories for any gratuitous cloak of legitimacy, Newcomb did with television what literature critics had been doing with books for thousands of years with poems and plays and, most recently, novels. He considered text and context; he responded with heart and head.

A year later, Newcomb, as editor, brought out the first edition of an anthology that marked a kind of first flowering of American television criticism. *Television: The Critical View* contained essays by humanities scholars, social scientists, and nonacademic free-lancers. The book was a tremendous success in the academic market, finding and filling a real need among a generation of students *and* teachers who were intimately familiar with television language, mythology, drama, and manners, but who, for lack of just such a book, could not "officially" consider this common culture in the print-oriented world of the classroom. The introduction of the VCR into the consumer appliance market at about this time did much to further promote the rise of academic television studies. Over the next ten years, increasing numbers of professors and students would have these machines at their personal disposal. During this same period, the "video reserve room" gradually became a common component of American college libraries. The videotape was gaining the accessibility, if not the respect, of the book.

Though the appearance of the Newcomb volumes seems almost by itself to have initiated a sudden and unexpected beginning for television criticism, it would be a mistake to think that such a wave of critical interest could have developed without regard to television content. There is a picture of Archie Bunker on the cover of *TV: The Most Popular Art* and there is good reason to believe that this character was not arbitrarily chosen over Lucy Ricardo, Sergeant Joe Friday, or Samantha the Witch. As Newcomb observed, the sitcom, after a long incubation as a static, banal genre, had only recently been "changed into a vehicle for biting social commentary" by shows such as *All in the Family, M*A*S*H,*

Maude, and *The Mary Tyler Moore Show*.[26] The genre's expansion into "hot" topics was probably the greatest magnet for the sudden critical attention. An interest in the dramatic concerns of situation comedies led to an interest in the people who were highlighting those concerns and who were thus expressing opinions about them. Identifiable television *auteurs* began to emerge from the indecipherable shadows of the final credits crawl. Norman Lear was the first non-performing TV personality to be granted the celebrity status of a *Playboy* interview.[27] The expansion of the sitcom's mimetic agenda accomplished by Lear, Larry Gelbart, and the MTM production team of James Brooks, Allan Burns, Ed Weinberger, and Stan Daniels had fertilized a critical field. As forgotten birthdays, fibs told by children, and reminders of dad's earthy wisdom gave way in the sitcom to abortions, racial epithets, and ironic commentary on the style of modern life, the national drama of prime-time television began to "create an audience" in much the sense that Seldes had hoped it would.

Indeed, after a quarter of a century of network television, *All in the Family* was the first weekly series to provoke sustained critical dialogue. Every racist, ethnocentric, sexist, and sexual preferentialist remark uttered by Archie Bunker seemed to elicit another newspaper column or magazine article during the early 1970s. Academic monographs soon followed. Political activists, clergy, and industry operatives joined reviewers, social scientists, and humanistic critics in a debate on the merits of the program. Some thought it a welcome airing of the nation's dirty laundry; others deplored the regrettable opening of a Pandora's box. The paradigm of "The Mass Culture Debate" had decisively shifted from "television vs. culture" to "good television vs. bad television." Moreover, by taking part in this dialogue, intellectuals were freely admitting in public that they were actually watching TV. A penchant for abstract theory was no longer a sufficient credential for a would-be critic of television; the grounding of theory in textual evidence was now required. It was not enough to summarily dismiss *All in the Family* as "dangerous" or as a "sublimation"; you had to know who Meathead was.

Lear spun off a string of sitcom hits from *All in the Family*, including *Maude, Good Times,* and *The Jeffersons,* each of which further intensified the suddenly volatile discourse of what had been thought to be among the most arid genres of an intellectually parched medium. In 1979, Richard Adler edited an anthology titled *All in the Family: A Critical Appraisal,* which was perhaps the first attempt at a comprehensive critical assessment of a weekly half-hour situation comedy. In 1984, the British Film Institute book series released *MTM: "Quality Televi-*

sion," a comprehensive anthological treatment of the aesthetic cosmology of an entire commercial production studio.

In *The Producer's Medium: Conversations with Creators of American TV* (1983), Horace Newcomb and Robert S. Alley offer ample evidence that this bursting forth of new energy in the post-1960s sitcom was anything but unselfconscious on the part of the artists who accomplished it. For example, Allan Burns, one of the co-creators of *The Mary Tyler Moore Show,* told Newcomb and Alley:

> We were feeling pretty good about it *(The Mary Tyler Moore Show),* cocky about it. We felt it was going to be *the* show. Then we sat down and watched (the pilot episode of) *All in the Family* and we came out with very mixed feelings. We were very impressed that something was going to be that competitive with us. To be be honest we thought it was going to steal a lot wind from our sails.[28]

Although Burns's apprehension was correct and *All in the Family,* with its unprecedented five years in the Nielsen number one spot, stole most of the headlines, *Mary Tyler Moore* and its spin-offs, *Rhoda* and *Phyllis,* managed to create a critical dialogue of their own, focusing on the changing image of the single working woman in American culture during a period when increasing numbers of women were seeking employment outside the home. Critical comment on *The Mary Tyler Moore Show* became de rigueur for women's magazines ranging from *Family Circle* to *Ms.* Similarly, Gelbart's *M*A*S*H,* with its pungent discourses on war and peace, individuality and bureaucracy, and relations between the sexes provoked popular and academic comment during (and since) its decade-long production run.

Seldes' argument that any popular TV show deserved serious critical attention just because it was popular had never really won partisans. But the new sitcoms of the early 1970s did win attention by directly addressing their content to political and social issues that were already on the minds of many writers and scholars. TV shows became reference points for public rhetoric, thus to some degree taking on the ideal progressive function of a national drama. By the end of the decade, the sitcom renaissance had spent itself. But diverse commentators had at last recognized television criticism as a powerful didactic tool: The practice outlived its initial catalyzing agent.[29]

A thorough understanding of the sudden proliferation of television criticism during the 1970s and 1980s also requires a look at certain technological and marketing stimuli that abetted the phenomenon. Beginning in the late 1960s, with corporate plans for satellite cable already off the drawing board, a conventional belief developed that cable TV would be the force that might finally break the oligarchic stranglehold of the networks on television programming. Unreconstructed cultural conservatives had long argued that the very "massness of" network television's "infinite" audience precluded quality. But cable seemed to address itself directly to this structural problem. Might not a multiplicity of channels, all aimed at groups smaller and more well-defined than the "mass," result in greater variety? Might not that greater variety, in turn, allow for the emergence of works of quality? Perhaps such works of quality would even provide standards for the entire medium: a rising tide to carry all boats. These optimistic predictions for cable television imagined secure places on the enlarged spectrum for classic and avant-garde art and for suppressed political points of view. The networks would surely continue their copshows and sitcoms, but all those new empty channels would just as surely allow room for the emergence of a video "high culture" that would be rooted in the historically "legitimate" paradigms that had been handed down through the literary arts.

This is not, however, exactly what happened. Cable TV did have a salubrious effect on television drama, but in a way that was not generally anticipated. Instead of taking the high road, the vast majority of cable services proved to be even less concerned with "quality" than the networks had been during their uncontested oligarchy. Exhibition "sports" such as professional wrestling and roller derby, long ago abandoned by ABC, CBS, and NBC, returned to American television—even to prime-time television—via cable. Theatrically released soft-core porno and gross-out films became staples of cable fare, even as the Big Three and then the Big Four were making concerted efforts to produce their own "issue-oriented" made-for-TV movies. New series, with such poor production values and such weak writing that they were easily recognizable as "subnetwork" appeared, including production revivals of long-dead network shows. The prime-time schedules of cable services such as USA or TBS can make ABC look like the BBC. Nick-at-Nite and the Family Channel (formerly the Christian Broadcasting Network) have presented entire prime-time line-ups consisting exclusively of reruns of precisely those 1950s sitcoms that had caused FCC Commissioner Newton Minow to coin the term "vast wasteland" in 1961.

The decades have turned the "vast wasteland" into "classic television." The Network TV Era (circa 1948–80) is emerging as a historically coherent cultural resource for twenty-first-century America—a rare commodity in a demographically balkanized culture bereft of a lucid religious or literary past. It is perhaps easiest to see this in Hollywood feature films. There is little profit in retelling the stories of Melville or Faulkner to an audience that has not been told these stories in the first place. *The Flintstones* and *The Fugitive*, two ABC shows from the 1960s, fit the bill much better in this regard. Having devoured and digested pre-television content, mass culture seeks nourishment from the marrow of pre-cable bones. Ah, the classics.

At the same time as their share of the total national audience began to diminish, the networks began focusing on the character, rather than the size, of their audiences. While university administrators sought greater cultural diversity for their inherently elite institutions, TV executives sought greater cultural uniformity for their inherently mass institutions. For thirty years, prime-time network programming had been dominated by the masscult doctrine of the "dead center," which held that the vanishing point of aesthetic and intellectual mediocrity was where the gold was buried. Also known as "least objectionability," this audience-gathering technique sought not so much to enlighten or entertain as to assemble by failing to offend. It was as if the Madison Avenue wisdom that success in sexual seduction could be achieved by suppression of body odors had been applied directly to the production of drama.

Saturday Night Live (NBC, 1975 to present) was among the first network programs to abandon this avant-garde technique in favor of the more traditional strategy of entertaining the audience. Even those who disliked *SNL* could not dislike it for the same reasons that they disliked *I Dream of Jeannie* or *The Brady Bunch*. The allusion-laden, often risqué, occasionally political comedy presented on *Saturday Night Live* by producer Lorne Michaels during the late 1970s violated every rule of "least objectionability" that had dominated broadcast TV since its McCarthy Era inception. Cable was coming; demographic segmentation had begun.

Perhaps the biggest breakthrough in prime-time "quality" came with the peculiar success of Steven Bochco's *Hill Street Blues*. Although *Hill Street*'s initial 1981 ratings were fatally low by traditional "mass" standards (the audience was estimated to be under ten million per week), NBC researchers discovered that among this meager mass could be found an astounding number of high-income viewers who had been to college and who, more importantly for network purposes, just might require the convenience of microwave ovens and autobahn cruisers for their painfully fast-paced lifestyles. Even better, the *Hill Street* viewer profile looked curiously like that of the typical pay-cable subscriber. MTM Enterprises, which had done so much to revitalize the sitcom and make it acceptable to upscale audiences, had now spawned a cop show capable of similar appeal.

Most critics loved *Hill Street Blues;* a few did not. But virtually no one could ignore this complex, well-crafted drama in a genre better known for one-dimensional characters, violent pyrotechnics, and twisted metal. The spectacle of high critical praise for a police series had been previously unthinkable. The fact that much of the adoration was based on formal innovations derived from afternoon soap operas made *Hill Street*'s critical reception all the more remarkable. The eventual commercial viability of the show paved the way for such series as *St. Elsewhere, L.A. Law, thirtysomething, Wiseguy,* and *Northern Exposure.* These shows, whose merits have been much debated individually, collectively broke the once immutable mold of traditional, symmetrical, good guy-bad guy comic book TV drama. All written from a point of view that helped to put the word "yuppie" into the language, these series are as much the revenge of articulate TV babies against *Starsky and Hutch, Marcus Welby, Perry Mason, Family,* and *The Untouchables* as they are the substance of what must be considered a middle-class public culture in America.

Television programs that are less patently "mass" and more identifiably "class" in orientation clearly get the lion's share of critical attention. The growing importance of authorship in critical studies of TV drama affirms the artistic gentrification of the medium by critics. While archival critical work on Network Era (i.e. masscult) *auteurs* and studios such as Paul Henning (*The Beverly Hillbillies, Green Acres,* et al.) or Mark VII Productions (*Dragnet, Adam-12,* et al.) remains relatively rare, there has been a steady stream of work on "class era" *auteurs* and studios such as Steven Bochco *(L.A. Law, NYPD Blue)* and MTM Enterprises *(Lou Grant, St. Elsewhere).* Work focusing on entire cable services, such as MTV, Black Entertainment Television, and the various religious channels has also proliferated.

To be sure, "The Mass Culture Debate" rattles on in the work of writers such as Neil Postman, Joshua Meyerowitz, and Gerry Mander. But the vital critical dialogues on American television that began with the Newcomb books have generally eschewed the old assumption that television is structurally doomed to aesthetic inferiority in comparison to "real" forms of art. The most important change brought about by the rise of television criticism is that blanket condemnations of the medium that make no distinction between works, authors, or genres, reveal themselves as bumptious. Any commentator making such assertions must admit that he or she is incapable of distinguishing between *M*A*S*H* and *McHale's Navy*, between *Law and Order* and *Silk Stalkings*, between *The Tracey Ullman Show* and *The Glen Campbell Goodtime Hour*, between *L.A. Law* and *Perry Mason*. (By the way, if you are not familiar with all these shows, that's understandable. Try to name eight novels that an audience of TV viewers has read. Still interested? Look them up in the *TV Guide* and watch the reruns.)

In each case, the "superior" program is not necessarily "objectively" obvious. That is a matter to be settled in the critical act. But a critic who cannot or will not make distinctions between works of the same genre or the same medium loses his or her credibility when issuing messianic warnings about the overall effects of a genre or medium. Such warnings are tedious echoes of the condemnations of the cinema that were issued from turn-of-the-century pulpits. If you wouldn't trust a theater critic who hasn't seen *Macbeth* or *My Fair Lady*, don't trust a TV critic who doesn't know the difference between *I Love Lucy* and *The Lucy Show*.

Has television drama matured to the point that we may now speak of "highcult," "midcult," and "masscult" programs? If so, what are the salient features that define these aesthetics? Issues such as self-reflexivity, moral ambiguity, and formal innovation are worth considering in this context. What are the implications of the "mass-to-class" evolution of television drama for the American social class structure? Are new media likely to follow a similar pattern of development? Will historians one day recall (with perhaps a twinge of democratic nostalgia) the period of "three-network television" when Americans of virtually all classes were watching much the same shows and possessed what might be termed "a national culture?" Will demographically targeted television services such as MTV (youth), Lifetime (women), and ESPN (men) produce programs in the familiar grammars of the historical network genres? Or will the mythic structures of the sitcom, the game show, and the talk show be exploded by audience specificity? And of course the critic still does well to consider the question that Gilbert Seldes always held himself responsible for: Is there anything good on?

1. As cited in William Boddy, *Fifties Television: The Industry and its Critics* (Urbana: Univ. of Illinois Press, 1993), 237.

2. The period known as "the golden age of television drama" is perhaps more well known as "the McCarthy era," a coincidence not discussed nearly often enough. For an illuminating study of the ideological conventions forced upon TV dramatists during "the golden age," see Kenneth Hey, "Marty: Aesthetics vs. Medium in Early Television Drama," in *American History/American Television*, ed. John E. O'Conner (New York: Ungar, 1983), 95–133.

3. See Daniel J. Czitrom, *Media and the American Mind* (Chapel Hill: Univ. of North Carolina Press, 1983). Czitrom describes an almost ritual pattern of response by American intellectuals to the introduction of new mass communications media.

4. Herbert Marcuse, *One-Dimensional Man* (Boston: Beacon Press, 1964), 101.

5. Gunther Anders, "The Phantom World of TV," trans. Norbert Guterman, *Dissent* 3 (1956): 14.

6. T. S. Eliot, "Notes Toward the Definition of Culture," in *Christianity and Culture* (New York: Harcourt 1968), see especially "Sect and Cult," 141–57.

7. Walt Whitman, Preface, *Leaves of Grass* (1855) ed. Malcolm Cowley, *Walt Whitman's Leaves of Grass* (New York: Penguin, 1976), 14.

8. Dwight Macdonald, "A Theory of Mass Culture," *Dissent 3*, reprinted in *Mass Culture: The Popular Arts in America*, ed. Bernard Rosenberg and David M. White (New York: Free Press, 1957), 62.

9. Michael Ross and Ernest van den Haag, *The Fabric of Society* (New York: Harcourt, Brace, 1957), 101.

10. In Rosenberg and White, *Mass Culture*, see David Manning White, "Mass Culture in America: Another Point of View," 13–21; and Melvin Tumin, "Popular Culture and the Open Society," 548–56.

11. Robert Sklar, *Movie-Made America: A Cultural History of American Movies* (New York: Random House, 1975), see especially Part I, "The Rise of Movie Culture."

12. For an argument of this thesis far more subtle than anything the Frankfurt boys every came up with, see J. Fred MacDonald, *Television and the Red Menace: The Video Road to Vietnam* (New York: Praeger, 1985).

13. See Boddy, *Fifties Television: The Industry and its Critics*, see especially Chapter 11, "The Honeymoon is Over: The End of Live Drama."

14. See bibliography for a representative sampling of J. Fred MacDonald's prolific work, including titles on racial representation, the political character of television drama, and a genre study of the Western.

15. George Lipsitz, "The Meaning of Memory: Family, Class and Ethnicity in Early Network Television Programs," *Cultural Anthropology* 1, no. 4 (November 1986), 355–87.

16. Thomas Cripps, "*Amos 'n' Andy* and the Struggle for Racial Integration," in *American History/American Television*, ed. John E. O'Conner, (New York: Ungar, 1983), 33–54.

17. Gilbert Seldes, "The 'Errors' of Television," *Atlantic* May 1937, 531–541.

18. See Walt Whitman, "Democratic Vistas, 1871," in *Demographic Vistas and Other Papers* (London: Walter Scott, 1888).

19. For a powerful treatment of this paradigm, see Sherman Paul, *Repossessing and Renewing: The Green Tradition in American Culture* (Baton Rouge: Louisiana State Univ. Press, 1978).

20. Gilbert Seldes, *The Seven Lively Arts*, (New York: Sagamore Press, 1957), 303.

21. Gilbert Seldes, *The Public Arts* (New York: Simon and Schuster, 1956), 161.

22. *The Jimmy Durante Show* (NBC, 1954–56; CBS, 1957) was part of *The Texaco Star Theatre* series. *The Donald O'Connor Show* aired on alternate weeks.

23. Gilbert Seldes, Review of *The Beverly Hillbillies*, TV Guide, (15 December 1962): 4.

24. Gilbert Seldes, *The New Mass Media: Challenge to a Free Society* (Washington, D.C.: Public Affairs Press, 1968), 98.

25. Horace Newcomb, *TV: The Popular Art* (New York: Doubleday, 1974).

26. Newcomb, *TV*, 57.

27. Barbara Cady and Norman Lear, "Playboy Interview: Norman Lear," *Playboy* 23 (Mar. 1976): 53–69.

28. Horace Newcomb and Robert S. Alley, *The Producer's Medium: Conversations with Creators of American TV*, (New York: Oxford, 1983), 174.

29. Another important aid in the facilitation of TV criticism, which I cannot treat adequately here, has been the increasing availability of reference texts. In the last ten years, dozens of books have been published that offer critics the bibliographic grunt work necessary for the easy practice of their art. Two of the most useful of these are Tim Brooks and Earle Marsh, *The Complete Directory to Prime-Time Network Television Programs* (New York: Ballantine, 1992), and Alex McNeil, *Total Television*, (New York: Penguin, 1984), both of which are massive compendiums of all types of program and industry data. Other reference works focus on more specific types of information, such as episode plot summaries for entire series, network scheduling histories, and biographical information on performers, production operatives, and industry executives.

"Totalitarian Stalinism and mass culture television were
typically depicted . . . as evil twin doubles . . ."

Eight Meditations on Couch Potato Stasis, Social Mobility, and the Itsy-Bitsy Attention Span Thing

Tiny Glances of Moral Suasion

During the 1950s American intellectuals typically worried that the greatest danger posed by the cultural administration of the entertainment-industrial complex was a suffocating blandness, a cheap beige sameness that would result from the relentless antisepticism of homogenized culture. Ah, but if it were only so. Walking the streets of the city of terror a half century later the specter of dullness seems like good clean fun; boredom, a vacation. But the regime of television presides over a cultural landscape that has developed into something more like a scorched and sleazy battleground: Holiday Inn, Beirut, not Holiday Inn, La Jolla.

Perhaps ever since its "discovery" America has always been a turf hosting gang wars—races, ethnicities, religions, and lifestyle affinity groups fighting each other for a piece of the virgin 'hood. But far from abating this destiny by turning the warring factions into a leveled nation of docile couch potatoes, television seems to have stimulated further wrack and division. Every salient demographic trait in the marketer's vocabulary has become a gang color. Each guerrilla band uses its weapons—money, guns, drugs, visual intimidation, formal or informal police forces—to terrorize the others. It became clear to me sometime around the sighting of my first gray hair that shelter had eclipsed food and clothing as the principal problem I am likely to face for the rest of my life. Is there a safe place for me to live, given my age, income, heritage, sexual orientation, and tastes in cable television? If such a place exists, must it be behind locked gates to avoid the violent wrath of people growing up with no scenario for obtaining the consumer goods that TV teases them for not having? Does my current retirement plan take into account the spiraling costs of personal security in the evolving media environment? Does yours? Write me care of this publisher; I have no 800 number.

Curiously, television likes to offer itself as the voice of reason in all this hysteria: a cultural referee presenting ameliorative dramatic descriptions of the chaos, urging mutual understanding and a sense of collective interest among the battling parties. The News, which serves as the oracular source of most television fiction as well as a genre in its own right, bends over backward to disdain the violence that is at the core of dramatic appeal. Those tiny glances of disgust thrown by the anchors as segués between atrocities are the most intense moments of moral suasion that television has thus far offered to its viewers. Or, as Kaufman and Colodzin observed in their book *Your Career in Television* (1950), "the lift of an eyebrow or the flash of a smile (is) more important than the sweep of an army." [1]

Yuppies: A Remembrance

The debut of the yuppie as a national archetype during the social destabilizations of the 1980s was an important event in the maintenance of America's mythological vision of itself as the land of social mobility. The move up the old post-Ellis Island ladder—from peasant to citizen farmer, from day laborer to skilled technician, from notions hawker to merchant, from wretched refuse of teeming shore to mortgage-paying opponent of sufficient taxation to keep the libraries open—had traditionally been catalogued as a family event, an historical thrust that boosted the fortunes of the next generation toward education, entrepreneurship, and the ever-greater pleasures of gratuitous consumerism.

But the yuppie was neither tired (unless suffering from Epstein-Barr syndrome), nor poor (though occasionally suffering cash-flow problems) nor particularly yearning to be any freer than a half-dozen credit cards could make a person. He, she, or it was, rather, a self-annointed instant aristocrat of consumerism. With enough disposable income to go on cruise-ship vacations, take karate lessons, or even set up a tax-advantaged college fund for 0.8 children if needs be, the yupster woke up in the Republican party's new morning for America not as a dynasty builder doing God's work, but rather as an unrepentant instant grat-brat, a selfconscious materialist emerging from an emphatically not-so-slimy pond of highly educated people who could do quite well, thank you, without either Marx or Jesus, but who really did have some use for Armani.

A yuppie, quite more to the point than being either young, urban, or professional, was a person who insisted by conspicuous display that his or her taste in mass culture was superior to your taste in mass culture. By eating three-dollar (one scoop!) ice cream cones that have umlauts in their brand names, by drinking water from Europe's polluted reservoirs in preference to our own, by driving cars whose aerodynamic designs and engine displacement ratios imply immunity from traffic law, the post-moralists on the 1980s seemed to believe that they could transcend the identity of nameless, faceless ciphers grazing in the center of the main herd by joining a highly visible—if still basically nameless and faceless—super-herd, grazing off to one side, over by the good grass. If such a metaphor seems too pastoral, this phenomenon can also be called by its business school name: target marketing.

Democracy, as sold to the public in a limitless blitz of TV, radio, and billboard spots, as implied by supermarket discount flyers and lottery games, as the content of slogans, symbols, and icons that are learned by rote before the thinking process is even exposed to the referants that originally inspired them, became a casualty during the Reagan presidency of a sensibility that aggrandized itself by its rejection of such democratic delights as cheap ice cream, free tap water, and Chevrolets. Muffins, si; donuts, no! Politics is just another aspect of culture. Common decency is, after all, *common*, and who in his or her elevated status wants that stuff, anyway?

At its pinnacle of wealth and power in the decades following the proof of its willingness to drop The Big One, the Federal government made considerable amends to its own unwashed classes for the excesses of the Depression. The G.I. Bill, the rise of solvent and federally insured savings and loan institutions, the extraordinary improvement of low-cost state university education, the Interstate Highway Act of 1956, and other such upwardly mobile goodies extended the bounty of bourgeois lifestyle deep into the class structure of the white nation.

Even those segments of society not specifically targeted for enhancements managed real, if more modest, benefits from the cornucopia of the Cold Peace. Blacks won a century-long fight to break the back of de jure Jim Crow discrimination in public (i.e., consumer) accommodations. Women won protections from the greatest excesses of de jure Victorianism. A highly educated homosexual middle-class, with an understanding of the lessons of the Nazi Holocaust nipping at its heels, began to seek citizenship rights in its own name. Wheelchair ramps appeared as if by court order. It seemed like everyone was trying to get into the act. No self-respecting dolphin was willing to end up as tuna on white.

But there is an old wisdom that reminds people—especially people who are nurtured on the intoxicating nectars of youthful privilege and who are beginning to experience the inevitable glooms of middle age—that it is hardly worth belonging to a country club that will admit anyone who wants to join it. The flip side of all the conspicuous displays of good taste that began haunting the "better" shopping malls of America during the Nancy years was an increasing disdain for those who are less aesthetically gifted. The flip side of an appreciation of those umlaut ice creams is a depreciation of the barbarians who actually eat *the supermarket store brand*. There is, regrettably, a well-worn path between the upscale section of the freezer case and radical reaction; it has been walked by the likes of Ezra Pound and Albert Speer.

"The most radical division . . . of humanity," wrote José Ortega y Gasset in 1932, "is that which splits it into two classes of creatures: those who make great demands on themselves, piling up difficulties and duties; and those who demand nothing special of themselves, but for whom to live is to be every moment what they already are, without imposing on themselves any effort toward perfection."[2] What might these latter creatures know of nouvelle cuisine? Let them eat Whoppers.

The yuppie said, "My taste is better than yours." There's nothing new in that. It's a behavior at least as old as money. Thorstein Veblen, to name the best example, made fun of the particular American variety of it in *Theory of the Leisure Class* (1899). But what was radical about the yuppie was that he or she said, sincerely, innocently, downright shamelessly, "My taste in mass-produced goods is better than your taste in mass-produced goods."

Fun With Communism

> Is it possible for a new Stalin to appear today who could murder people? In an era of computers and satellite TV . . . it's impossible.
>
> Lech Walesa

During a kindergarten-to-graduate-school public education in New York City, I could not help but manage to learn that the two greatest menaces to the humanities (and therefore humanity) in the second half of the twentieth century were a pair of post-industrial abominations known as Stalinism (the political threat) and television (the cultural threat). Administered for the most part by devotées of Adlai Stevenson and the nineteenth-century European novel, this education was extraordinarily effective in anticipating each next step of its own process. It has been less useful, however, as a tool for understanding the collapse of European Communism.

Totalitarian Stalinism and mass culture television were typically depicted on the blackboard as evil twin doubles joined at the heart by their mutual disdain for the best that has been thought and said by white men west of the Urals. A single social democratic blow, struck some day by the indomitable if sometimes lazy invisible hand of the Enlightenment, would end both the political hegemony of Communism in the Warsaw Pact nations and the cultural hegemony of consumerism in NATO. The Comrades would win freedom of assembly and line right up to see Ibsen; the Comrades would win freedom of speech and jump into heated debates about Tolstoy and Kafka; the Comrades would win freedom of religion and become zealous congregants at the church of secular humanism. The Audience, meanwhile, would be granted freedom from sitcoms; they would sign up for the Molière Channel, whose price would be subsidized by tax money.

The promoters of this mythic scenario—the usually vociferous intellectuals who occupy the narrow American demoralized zone between bleeding heart liberalism and bleeding wallet neoconservatism—have had little to say about the spectacle of one of the twin brutes getting the pinfall over the other. There is reason to suspect that at least some of these partisans of the extreme center would have preferred the spectacle of the members of the politburo wiping the floor with the TV execs. In any case, television has emerged as a vital tool in the remarkable dismantling of the old police-state apparatuses in the Second World, and this unexpected development has left the cult of Lionel Trilling at an uncharacteristic loss for words.

Thomas B. Rosenstiel, who writes on foreign affairs for the *Los Angeles Times,* got quite to the point in a January 1990 essay on this subject when he noted that the fall of the Eastern bloc regimes had made "1989 . . . the year George Orwell proved wrong. Television it turned out, is not the ultimate tool of repression . . . Orwell's mistake in his novel *1984* was thinking that television exercises control by inflicting pain. Maybe, as Aldous Huxley suggested, TV controls by inflicting pleasure." (Actually Neal Postman wrote the same exact thing in 1985 in

Amusing Ourselves to Death, but as a service to readers I have tried to carefully measure the use of his prose.)

For almost half a century, the political freedoms guaranteed by the Magna Carta, the U.S. Constitution, and the Declaration of the Rights of Man were waved at the people of the people's republics. Thousands responded individually by dodging bullets, crawling under barbed wire, and making their way through the muck of sewers and drain pipes. Some of them sacrificed their lives in the effort. But the utopian legends of the print world were simply not compelling enough to break the inertia of totalitarian order. It was only when TV waved stereos and VCRs, blue jeans and hamburgers, automobiles and dishwashers, HBO and CNN, toilet paper and relief from B.O., across a curtain constructed of such a flimsy nineteenth-century material as iron, that millions responded collectively. That freedom of the press stuff sounds great, but I want my MTV . . .

The failure of Communism to beat Capital to the communications punch is too ironic for novels. Those who professed to believe that history was a scientifically knowable material process were the ones who got caught with their technological pants down. They froze communications history at their own greatest moment of triumph—the world of the mimeograph machine and the bullhorn—and fetishized the immediate conditions that brought them to power as universal and eternal. On the other hand, those who claimed no wider earthly mission than trying to make a buck demonstrated the imagination to go with the flow. Lenin is supposed to have said, "the last Capitalist will sell us the rope with which to hang him." It seems more likely that the last Communist will be cancelled during the third hour of a speech on agricultural policy to the Young Pioneers annual convention.

Marshall You Can Drive My Car

"The talk about the American car as a status symbol has always overlooked the basic fact that it is the power of the motorcar that levels all social differences, and makes the pedestrian a second-class citizen," Marshall McLuhan wrote in his essay, "Motor Car: The Mechanical Bride." "Many people have observed that the real integrator of white and Negro in the South was the private car . . . not the expression of moral points of view. The simple and obvious fact about the car is that, more than any horse, it is an extension of man that turns the rider into a superman. It is a hot, explosive medium of social communication."[3]

When I moved from Boston to Los Angeles in 1989, I began to recognize both the prescience and innocence of McLuhan's remarks on automobile and ego. His presumption that a means of personal transportation may serve as a medium of personal communication is itself hardly revolutionary. A good sedan chair moving through the center of an oasis surely advertised at least as much about its passenger as a good sedan proclaims to fellow travelers while waiting at a red light or cruising the Interstate.

But in some ways McLuhan's vision of abundant car ownership as a democratizing force seems dated. Perhaps at one time the owning of a car in the United States did seem like the crossing of a Jordan River into the promised land of mass culture. But that was before the grand luxury of personal transportation had been degraded by modern planning into a necessity. Once the heady illusion of mastery crashed into the depressing reality of captivity, it was perhaps inevitable that a new pecking order of BMWs and Chevies and Toyotas would emerge to remind us that in creating the mass mind, anxiety is our most important process.

In Los Angeles, where shoeshine stands have parking lots and jay-walking is a severely and oft-punished crime, the forms and functions of the car and of urban life have become virtually indistinguishable. Could this really be me, I wonder, crawling in traffic from one part of downtown to another at three-thirty on a Tuesday afternoon in a city of millions with no subway system worth mentioning? All commerce and pleasure shall cease next Thursday for the sabbath of a tune-up. I have already developed a taste for restaurants that feature ample parking. I am beginning to cultivate similar criteria for choosing my friends.

I used to wash my car at the Lechmere U-Wash It in Somerville about three or four times a year—always in winter and always with the practical intention of saving the body from salt rot. Now, having been told more than once by unsmiling neighbors that my car is "looking kind of dirty," I take it regularly to The Carwash of the Stars, where illegal aliens in blue labcoats scoff at my bottom-of-the-line Volkswagen, while it sits, like some poor relation, among its opulent Teutonic cousins. This actually makes me defensive enough to overtip.

Spending so much time behind the wheel these days, I find that driving, perhaps as much as television, claims a sizable share of aesthetic shelf space in the supermarket of consciousness: much of it, no doubt, at the expense of books and other printed matter. The excitement of "reading" the world through the windshield—a world full of all kinds of possibilities, including elegance, pathos, mechanical breakdown, spontaneous consummation of consumer urge, and even sexual scrimmage—can be highly stimulating, a seamless web of cubist experience. In Los Angeles, where doughnut shops are shaped like doughnuts and hot dog stands like hot dogs, the driver, even on the way to work, can be overcome by the sensation of paying a visit to a kind of high-tech theme park: Late Capitalism World—please keep your windows rolled up and your air conditioning on.

The advantage of the car over the book or the TV set as a source of aesthetic experience is that it allows the user to simultaneously penetrate the world and keep it at bay. Reading and watching TV, though often thought of as antagonistic activities, are actually bound to each other as proscenium experiences. The dangers of these forms of recreation are merely psychological. But driving reinvolves an entire set of primitive alarms and reflexes that must have added much to the excitement of our ancestors' early jogs through the jungle. Any driver must live behind the knowledge that the windshield, despite its shatter-proof guarantee, is a proscenium that may be cracked at any moment without warning. Sensory phenomena continually compete for the driver's attention and fracture it. Architecture, topography, weather, and proximity to the sociopathic or insane all can make dents in drive-time consciousness.

I grew up in New York City, where generations of college students read and re-read Kant's *Critique of Pure Reason* on the two-hour subway ride from Brooklyn to Columbia University. In Los Angeles, special time must be arranged for the reading of the city's only major daily newspaper. While the humanities cower behind the study of printed literatures and histories, the physical education department offers courses on the epistemology of the future. Who will be so bold as to presume to discern the world without driver's education?

That's Postmodernism For You

With less than a decade left to go in the millennium, scientists are choosing up sides for the various competitions among new ways to destroy the world and new ways to save it from destruction. Social scientists guard the public welfare by frenetically keeping tabs on the effects of these doomsday sprints upon the consumption habits of the audience. And where is the critical imagination of the humanities in all of this? Struggling to define postmodernism, of course. Ever since God ceased to play a primary role in the study of art it has become a required course in the humanities to cordially entertain the mortifying possibility that being germane is as likely to be a meaningless waste of time as not.

So let the scientists argue the toxicity of aspartame and global warming. Let the social scientists render their demographic daguerreotypes of ice cream eaters in the age of frozen yogurt and the TV viewing habits of convicted felons. The fecund spring earth of the humanities pleads to be tilled by a different type of farmer: there are icy one-liners on unread books just ripe for the repeating; there are expressions of pious exasperation to be made at the carnival of horrors that passes for the daily news; there are jealous resentments about how much money everybody else makes to be shared in the communion of righteous indignation. We have our own poisons to bury in our own frozen yogurts.

Dream this: you are at a bad-wine-and-bad-cheese reception after a dreadful poetry reading (the verse was too mannered for authentic passion). With no gender or sexual preferentialist prejudices implied, you meet a human being, who though first and foremost a human being of course, is an object of desire. This Other, you learn, actually *liked* the poetry. But who said this was a perfect world? When stands the penis, as the old expression goes, falls the head. (Whoops, I'm getting gender specific.) So, as Joel says of his dream in *Risky Business,* you go with it. After all, the very act of writing poetry in the twentieth century, or at least since Auschwitz and Hiroshima, is arguably courageous in and of itself, no? Check *The New York Review of Books,* any issue. Having neatly resolved a dilemma of taste with an unimpeachable moral generalization, what now? What if, just what if, the Other thought that you had a workable and concise definition of postmodernism? It couldn't exactly hurt your chances . . .

Try this (just give the footnote to love): Well, modernism, of course was the culmination of the long-held Western precept that art is an imitation of nature. Now perhaps that rang true in Aristotle's day and even in Shakespeare's. Zola, without doubt, took it as an article of faith well into the nineteenth century, even as he attempted to reinvent literature as a didactic social science. But you can't tell me that things haven't changed. What Freud called "psychology" at the turn of the century seems more like applied rear-guard literary criticism these days.

Don't quote me on this but the spiral of technology has increasingly removed us from contact with nature, so that now a child is more likely to be intimate with the waves of televisual representation than with the ones rolling in off the ocean. As the ancient FM poet Joni Mitchell once sang, "They took all the trees and put 'em in a tree museum/And they charged all the people a dollar-and-a-half just to see 'em/Oo, oo." Having lost firsthand contact with nature ("the model"), how can we possibly judge a rendering of it ("art")?

Well, don't forget that the artist, as much as the viewer, is a product of this removed-from-nature, technologically generated environment. So, isn't it merely logical to understand the artist's rendering as not some imitation of nature, but rather as an edited collage of preprocessed units? Should we not conclude that previous artifice—rather than nature—has become the primary model for the imagination? Wake up and smell the decaf, folks. Take a peak out the electronic window. Are we living in something that looks more like a garden or a junkyard? New form can only be forged from the materials at hand. Don't mourn, recontextualize! It's fun and there's even an ecologically sound metaphor to support it: the recycling of consciousness.

But the night is still young; the Other takes an unimpressed sip of the bad white wine and requests an example. Reification? That's valid. You whimsically dip a carrot stick into nonfat yogurt dressing and cite one.

Take Mao Zedong, remember him? (He used to spell his name differently.) His observation that "all political power grows out of the barrel of a gun" seems not so much groundless as weightless in the age of infotainment, *n'est-ce pas?* But I digress. A former school teacher, the Chairperson apparently liked to think of himself as a didactic ideologue who was dedicating progressive applications of Marxist-Leninist analysis to the harsh realities of twentieth-century Chinese peasant-cum-proletarian life. But to get this picture of Mao, the contemporary student of history would probably have to kill a day or several at the library either reading books or looking at scratchy black-and-white 16-mm documentaries that play classical music on the soundtrack, or both.

Television, on the other hand, tends to remember Mao as a man so au courant during his "fifteen minutes" that the very style of the suit he wore came to bear his name. Though Mao may have spent much of his actual (or "natural") life studying, plotting, writing, shooting, pondering issues of agricultural policy, and so on, he is retained for us in collective external memory as a newsblip on CNN, a video cartridge popped in for this or that occasion. He is background material for a breaking China news story or for a piece of sixties nostalgia; on a slow day, his birthday or deathday might even justify itself. Giant pictures of him are held high by the crowds marching through Tiananmen Square: Oh yes, Mao Zedong, the Grand Marshall of the Long March, presiding over a May Day parade featuring Communists in the days when communists were Communists.

The obsolete modernist craves facts about Mao and about the historical context of his life, believing that these will, in rigorous synthesis, yield a satisfying conclusion, which can confidently—even proudly—be called the truth. But the postmodern sensibility simply accepts the images that have survived of Mao, preferring the visceral stimulation of a needle shower of factoidal associations to the dubious (and sometimes dangerous) pretension of "The Truth."

Now tell me about your set. What premium services are featured in your package?

Uses for the Novel

I have made a practice during the last several years of asking students in graduate courses to try to come up with the name of a novel that every member of the class has read. I try to do this on the first day of class, with the idea that someone will come up with a title before the semester is over. Some students are amused by the idea and come to class with suggestions over the next week or two. All kinds of things surface. The student who majored in literature as an undergraduate manages stupified outrage because not a single student in the class has ever read a book or even a short story by James Joyce. The best-seller fan can't believe that there are living, breathing people in the world who have never read a Stephen King or Jackie Susann tome. "Don't they make you read *Moby Dick* or *The Scarlet Letter* or *Huckleberry Finn* in high school?" I chime in, just to keep up my end of the conversation. An apparent sense of generational defensiveness sometimes emerges, leading a sophisticate to ask whether "new journalism" books count as novels. I revel over the fact that I have lived to see a legitimate issue in contemporary literary criticism raised by a student in my classroom. I skip the particulars and say okay. But we still can't come up with a winner; just a couple of gonzo-ites who are "totally amazed" that college graduates walk the

American earth who have never grooved to the prose of Hunter S. Thompson, Joan Didion, or Tom Wolfe.

Thus far, neither I nor any of the students in any of about a dozen or so graduate classes (I wouldn't even attempt this in an undergraduate course) has come up with even one title that everyone in the room has read. In fact, students increasingly treat the question as a hostile put down designed by Herr Doktor Professor to prove their lack of *Kultur*. As my pathetic need for approval actually seems to expand with age, it becomes increasingly difficult to continue this dangerous research.

In any case, lacking a true answer to this cultural puzzle, there is a relative leader, a novel that often comes close—sometimes within one or two in a class of fifteen: *The Great Gatsby* by F. Scott Fitzgerald. Short, spunky, romantic, based on misguided love, climaxing in two violent deaths, and, perhaps most significant of all, less than a hundred and twenty pages even in a large type edition, *Gatsby* seems to qualify as the kind of high culture novel about which it can be said with a confident lack of pretension, "The book is better than the movie" (in this case either of the movies—and it's true). As a result of its relatively universal popularity in the age of demographic target cultures, I even try to use it in my writing when I can.

Nick Carraway, Fitzgerald's socially weary and morally decent narrator, cannot help but mock the behavior of Tom Buchanan, whose personality constantly vacillates between the polarities, as Nick puts it, of "prig and libertine." Tom, who is married to Nick's cousin Daisy, is a Mayflower millionaire from Chicago. He is quick to rant on about threats to the integrity of the nuclear family and about the evils of bootlegging. He even decorates his white supremacist theories in a collage of genetic and Puritan pieties. Having produced nothing himself, he tells Nick, "We've produced all the things that go to make civilization—oh, science and art, and all that. . . . If we don't look out the white race will be—utterly submerged. . . . It's up to us, who are the dominant race, to watch out or these other races will have control of things."

And yet somehow, without blinking an eye, Tom also maintains a mistress, whom he occasionally slugs, and drinks contraband whiskey with impunity. By the end of the novel, this defender of civilization even manages to become the willing accomplice to hit-and-run manslaughter (the killing, no less, of a white woman!).

There is something quintessentially American about Tom Buchanan's colorful internal contradictions. Phillip Rahv called it "paleface vs. redskin"; Sherman Paul called it "gray vs. green." After all, aren't Tom's the frictions produced by the same cultural paradigm that spawned such unlikely pairs as slavery and the Bill of Rights, Anthony Comstock and H. L. Mencken, Prohibition and rock 'n' roll? The Puritans fled to America so they could live as Christian ascetics only to find that they needed the decadent corruptions of Europe to give meaning to the their stoicism. Way across the ocean, with no one but bonafide heathens to keep an eye on them, they felt compelled to make life so unbearable for themselves that they eventually stopped being the Puritans—or did they? At the same time, there were Europeans who came to America with the idea of living free in the woods. Many of them ended up at liberty to mow lawns in suburban subdivisions.[4]

Chapters of this tale of two psyches are still being written. School boards ban the "pornographic" novels of J. D. Salinger and Mark Twain, while their own children can hardly find a way to hide from the daily video displays of violence and sexual abuse that fuel the engine of American commerce.

American marketers cherish their constitutionally protected freedom of expression. Should artists be granted similar freedom of expression? The National Endowment for the Arts finds itself in the embarrassing position of being the national school board, taking the heat from the angry parents, especially the righteous fathers of Congress. As Rod Serling might put it, submitted for your mytho-American approval: one Jesse Helms. Tobacco? Yes—a matter of individual freedom. AIDS education? No—a matter of public morality. Clean needles for addicts? Ditto. An advocate of democracy who wraps himself in the American flag and uses racist TV commercials against his opponent in a Senate election. A self-annointed defender of the U.S. Constitution who advocates limitations on freedom of personal expression. Perhaps Walt Whitman, a poet who might be facing serious funding problems himself these days, had Helms—and Tom Buchanan—in mind when he wrote, "That America necessitates new standards for her poetry is such a point with me that I never tire of dwelling on it."[5]

At least until the 1960s, the threat to decency was seen as originating exclusively from below, in the grimy precincts of popular culture. The lurid tabloids and cheap peek-a-boo entertainments that were multiplying across the shelves of the late nineteenth-century culture market were a clear and present challenge to Victorian propriety. Some of this still goes on, as with the occasional attempt to boycott a TV show (such as *Married . . . With Children* or *Beavis and Butthead*), but the real action in the "let's save our children from culture" movement today is shifting toward a front on the higher ground. No sitcom boycott has ever stirred anything like the reactions to Helms's attack on the Maplethorpe and Serrano exhibitions. The danger to civilization it seems is no longer lurking in the lower depths of *The Police Gazette, Captain Billy's Whiz Bang,* the Flora-Dora Girls, or the pool room, but hiding instead in the fortress of high culture—in the stuff stashed in the vaults of museums, universities, and institutional collections. Conservatives defending the masses from "high culture?" Walt Whitman, you are a genius.

Fitzgerald, as well as T. S. Eliot, José Ortega y Gasset, R. P. Blackmur, and other artists and intellectuals had realized by the 1920s that "high culture," the modern remnant of the old court culture of feudal Europe, no longer presided over society. They were genuinely alarmed—even, as in the case of Fitzgerald, moved to nihilism—by the realization that if high culture was to survive at all in the twentieth century, it would be by the forebearance of mass culture, which might throw it a few crumbs . . . well, just because it was so "classy." This is the indignity suffered by Fitzgerald in Hollywood that led to his crack-up. Faulkner avoided it by taking his drinking problem to a university sinecure—now the American road most often taken.

Masscult has been, in effect, taxing itself voluntarily to keep high-cult in business for the past half century. Contributions, either corporately or privately donated, from General Electric, CBS, Mobil Corporation, the U.S. government, and other institutions whose fortunes are rooted in mass culture consumerism, keep the symphonies, libraries, museums, ballets, studio theaters, cinema festivals, and noncommercial television and radio networks of this country afloat in the stormy laissez-faire ocean.

This is not easy for most devotees of *les beaux artes* in America to swallow. How would you like to be told that the complex, subtle and mythologically sanctioned genteel pleasures of your *boeuf Bourguignon* are privileges that come to you at the mercy of a tax on bubble gum—a piece of nutritionless plastic that impacts negatively on dental health and promotes bad manners? And furthermore, the more bubble gum chewed by the peasants, the richer the gourmet feast.

Up until now, most reminders of this distasteful arrangement have been hidden on the credits crawls of PBS television shows and in the fine print of theater and concert hall programs. But that may be changing. With the censor's eye pointed upscale, the big institutions (the NEA being perhaps the first) have to think harder about the newly politicized implications of supporting high culture, which had once been

such a safe charity. Just as corporate sponsors had to carefully examine sitcom scripts and variety shows acts for potential political con-
troversies during the 1950s, contemporary corporate sponsors may
have to give equal scrutiny to productions of *An Enemy of the People*
or *le Sacre du Printemps* or painting exhibitions at the Whitney or
adaptations of E. M. Forster novels. In that case tenured university
professors will have achieved full control of the nonprofitable arts
and the survival of the humanities will have truly become an academic
question.

I Thought of Nancy

The Trickle-Down Theory, an economic scheme that can trace its
roots to the medieval practice of throwing unwanted food over the walls
of castles and monasteries to provide divine bounty for starving peasants,
made an impressive comeback in the United States during the 1980s.
If nothing else, it proved that abstract theory can have an effect on
the so-called "real world." How else might ketchup have become a
vegetable?

Public education has been affected even more radically than condi-
ment classification. Once a dynamo of upward mobility, the American
school sits rusting in a graffiti-covered junkyard, a pathetically cheap
Chevette unable to compete with the frugal Toyotas and solid Mercedes
that rule the road. Teachers are laid off as class sizes increase. Schools
cut out "extra-curricular" activities, such as student newspapers and
drama productions. Public libraries trim their hours—in some ways the
unkindest cuts of all. Meanwhile, with only a "trickle" of their profits
dripping "down," those upstanding citizens with decent credit ratings
(along, of course, with the plain old rich) wearily and philosophically
cover family education costs running into the tens of thousands of dollars
for the best prep schools and God-knows-what anymore for private
colleges.

It became profoundly unfashionable to discuss economic inequities
in polite company during the eighties. So let me move quickly to a more
genteel concern: culture, which is always in fashion. It is in this area that
America has surpassed the fantasies of supply-side economists with some
impressive trickling down. For about a century and a half now, significant segments of the educated classes have been accepting (in some cases
even reading) Charles Darwin, and taking his trickle-up theories of biology as an indication that God either doesn't exist or is dead or perhaps
just doesn't care much about how humans behave anymore. During this

period, ever greater numbers of people with smarts and money have felt more free to focus their attentions on what had previously been known, with some contempt, as carnal hedonism. The prerogatives of degeneracy have been somewhat democratized.

True ideologues of Free Love, including such turn-of-the-century American radicals as Thorstein Veblen and Gertrude Stein, made examples of their lives in this regard, defiantly extoling the virtues of visceral pleasure in the face of a cosmic void. By the 1920s, according to writers such as Dorothy Parker and F. Scott Fitzgerald, goodly numbers of the well-born were casually taking drugs, engaging in non-marital sex and living on credit, assuming instant gratification as their birthright.

With the promise of paradise seemingly lost, the white avant-gardists of the Roaring Twenties went slumming in places such as Harlem and the South Side of Chicago, looking for tips from the economically misera-ble on how to live happily that might be applied to their own private brand of spiritual misery. All this upper-class naughtiness usually gets a glamorous write-up in the history books as "The Jazz Age." But while all this was happening, the ham-and-eggers weren't even allowed a legal glass of beer.

It was not until the 1960s that the culture of heroic hedonism, bor-rowed from the permanent underclass and exquisitely remodeled by the permanent overclass, had seeped both up and down to the middle realm of the check-in desk at the Holiday Inn. If automobiles, air travel, and stereophonic audio equipment were not to be restricted to the rich in a democratic society, neither, it turns out, could marijuana, cocaine, or quickie divorces. Could Timothy Leary have guessed that tune-in, turn-on and drop-out would devolve into addictive personalities, functional illiteracy, and crack babies? Could Henry Ford, perhaps the Timothy Leary of the twenties, have known that his Model T, in addition to giving the "common man" unprecedented freedom of movement, might one day become his most lethal murder weapon?

When Nancy Reagan, who apparently enjoys saying yes to plenty, said, "Just say no," was she talking to Baudelaire? Coleridge? Blake? Poe? Charlie Parker? Allen Ginsberg? Andy Warhol? Or is this a proviso reserved for the nine-to-fivers—those who might be late for work if they get too stoned?

At the end of *The Great Gatsby*, Gatsby and Myrtle, the two lower-class characters with upper-class aspirations, are left dead as a result of the self-centered hedonistic excesses of Tom and Daisy, a super-rich couple. "They were careless people, Tom and Daisy," wrote Fitzgerald, "they smashed up things and creatures and then retreated back into their money or their vast carelessness, or whatever it was that kept them together, and let other people clean up the mess they had made." The Toms and Daisies, so visible throughout the eighties, have made their retreat since the Gulf War. But they smashed up things pretty good during the 1980s. Can Bill and Hillary do any better?

How Darwin, Marx, Freud, Sally Jesse, Geraldo, and Oprah Have Helped Keep the Menendez Brothers and Lorena Bobbitt Out of Jail

Sometime during the late 1960s, when the permanent crime wave first began, "law and order" emerged as a conservative buzz slogan for everything from the repression of antiwar and civil rights demonstrations to the abrogation of the rights of the accused. It helped elect Richard Nixon president, twice, and of course this turned out to be an extraordinary irony. Since that time, "law and order" has come to evoke a kind of utopian vision of a society where a person could actually go for a walk after dark, perhaps even unarmed, in a major metropolitan area of the United States.

You would think that in a society so desperately yearning for "law and order" it would be pretty easy to get a courtroom conviction on, say, two men who entered their parents' home and murdered their unarmed mother and father, lied about it, and then admitted doing it. Or that a woman who cut off her husband's penis might do some pretty stiff jail time. Or that a convicted felon would not stand a chance at getting a major party's nomination for the U.S. Senate in a conservative state. Or that an ice skater who admitted withholding information from the police would have a hard time getting a spot representing that nation at the Olympics. But then you would have to think again.

When it comes to personal physical safety, "law and order" is a paramount concern, and this is certainly how it should be. This yearning is fully extended into the area of property rights, and that too makes perfect sense. But when it comes to crimes that don't randomly threaten the public's person or property, Americans are proving themselves capable of demonstrating a high level of deeply enlightened understanding —a sensitivity to human motivation and frailty that would impress Jean-Jacques Rousseau. Unlike the "animals" of the underclass, white middle-class people view their fellow white middle-class people as complex creatures whose actions can only be explained by the logics of human behaviorial science.

How did this come about? The thrust of much nineteenth-century intellectual activity was to rationalize subjects that had been shrouded in religious mysticism for millenia. Science replaced Latin as the sacred language of truth. Darwin turned the creation of the human race into the study of *biology*. Freud turned the mysteries of sexual sin into *psychology*. Marx dismissed "the invisible hand" of Adam Smith and divine will as factors in economics in favor of what his followers have liked to call *scientific* socialism. For a hundred years since, intellectuals have agonized over these paradigms. Some reconstituted long-held religious beliefs; others abandoned religion completely.

There is a theory that in a mass communications culture ideas that are at first only of interest to the elite will eventually trickle down to the population at large. The humming engines of the masscult factories face a relentless need for fresh fuel. "All," as Dwight Macdonald put it, "is grist for the mill." The talk show industry stripmines the intellectual landscape in its all-out search for raw materials. So today bargain-basement versions of Darwin, Freud, Marx, the nature vs. nurture debate and the whole kit-and-kaboodle of post-Enlightenment thinking are diffused coast-to-coast daily by Sally Jesse, Geraldo, Oprah, and anyone else with a first name and a distribution deal.

The chief message of these intellectual democrats seems to be that when people commit crimes that aren't random stick-ups or indiscriminate murder sprees, they are simply acting out logical responses to their personal experiences as abused victims. If the source of their abuse is not always obvious at first, it can be found. To be a modern progressive viewer of these programs you must accept the principle that evil does not exist and that people who commit hideous acts of violence (previously listed exceptions noted) are helplessly reacting to stimuli in their environment. They are sick. You would not send a person to jail for catching the flu, would you?

So while gangsta rappers are castigated in the halls of Congress for inciting the public to violence, talk show hosts reap hefty rewards by flattering their audiences with the news that they can do no wrong. We are all victims of abuse. We will all react to our abuse accordingly. Let's not be too hard on our fellow victims. Let's save that special hardness for the muggers. Three strikes and they're out.

1. As cited in William Boddy, *Fifties Television: The Industry and its Critics*, 83.
2. José Ortega y Gasset, "The Coming of the Masses," reprinted in *Mass Culture: The Popular Arts in America,* ed. Bernard Rosenberg and David Manning White (New York: Free Press, 1957), 43.

3. Marshall McLuhan, *Understanding Media: The Extensions of Man* (New York: Signet, 1964), 198.

4. See Hawthorne's "The Maypole of Merry Mount" in *Twice-Told Tales* for an epic account of the battle between American id and super-ego. Based on a true story!

5. Walt Whitman, "A Backward Glance on My Road," *Democratic Vistas and Other Papers* (London: Walter Scott, 1888), 99.

". . . montage reigns as the vital aesthetic feature
of American popular culture."

Distribution Is Everything

An Endless Decay of Standards

As television continues to mutate away from the acknowledged dramatic forms that it adapted from stage, screen, and radio during its genesis, even the stodgiest English teachers may one day look back upon the shows of the Network Era with a respectful fondness, much as they now pine for the "literateness" of the Studio Era genre movies that a previous generation of stodgy English teachers so throughly despised. At least in those primitive (classical?) days, when changing the channel meant a stroll across the room, viewers attended whole stories for dozens of minutes at a time. At least Aristotle's prescription that a drama have "a beginning, a middle, and an end" was respected, even if, to the tutored eye, ineptly or insanely. The ancient TV shows, media historians might someday remind us, actually made use of such time-honored devices as setting, characterization, conflict, and climax. Can the same be said for music videos, video games, or video grazing? Five-hundred-channel cable-TV may make the *literati* nostalgic for *Perry Mason;* unlimited fiber-optic capacity may well have them begging for *Laverne and Shirley.* Norman Lear already elicits the awe reserved for an old master among the pre-Nintendo boomers who pay the dues that keep the National Education Association in business.

Despite, or perhaps because of, the great audience's continuing devotional affection for commercially segmented narrative series reruns, the primacy of naturalistic plot construction—as it developed in the novel and the feature film over the course of two centuries and climaxed on Network Era television—is rapidly passing from the center stage of American popular culture.[1] Even theatrically released Hollywood blockbusters are put in the can devoid of the traditional meat-and-potato

129

elements of plot, a reflection perhaps of their larger market destiny as TV software.

Steven Spielberg's *Jurassic Park* (1993) is a stunning example of this, a special effects display that carries a story around in its back pocket just in case anybody might still be asking for one. Similarly, in the feature-film adaptation of Quinn Martin's ABC television series *The Fugitive* (1993), the most interesting scene in the movie—the spectacular bus crash and train wreck—occurs during the first fifteen minutes, after which the audience sits in the theater for the better part of two hours watching the unfolding of a "thriller," the ending of which has already been revealed to it, at home, a hundred times in syndication.

While watching Dr. Richard Kimball's safe return to the black-tie, penthouse life from which he was mistakenly plucked, I couldn't help but remember the ending of Mervyn Leroy's *I Am a Fugitive from a Chain Gang* (1932). In that quaint, old, pre-postmodern chestnut the wrongly accused, an architect, sneaks through the darkness toward the woman he loves. "How will you live?" she asks him. "I'll steal." The End.

Black-and-white era sitcom concepts such as *The Addams Family, The Beverly Hillbillies, Dennis the Menace,* and *Car 54, Where Are You?* are rehabilitated as collective memory conjures—organizing principles for marketing campaigns. They are abstract films in the sense that they have no discernible stories to tell. What an old network sitcom does possess is a commercial track record. A model for predicting the box office performances of these films can be fabricated from their Nielsen files, giving producers something to take to the bankers to secure production loans. Like the fashions of another era, old sitcoms can be taken out of the closet, cleaned, pressed, and sent down the runway one more time, instantly distinguishing themselves from the ubiquitous styles that have since evolved. Like a thirty-year-old Plymouth stopped at a red light, the peculiarities of *Dennis the Menace*'s archaic design allow it to stand out from the crowd and catch the public's eye, something neither the car nor the comedy could do while still in assembly-line production.

When the critical glass seems half full, this kind of a-narrative or quasi-narrative film construction may pass for radical postmodern form; at half empty, such films suggest a remarkable failure at the traditional crafts of drama production. Velocity, the remnant of what was once called pacing, has taken precedence over all other features of dramatic structure. The lifetime it takes to master a mythologically or religiously based poetic gave way to the dozen hours it takes to read a novel . . . gave way to the two-hour feature film . . . gave way to the sixty or thirty-minute broadcast episode . . . gave way to the three-minute video . . . gives way to the several seconds it takes to absorb an image, tire of it, and hit the remote control button for another. In ironic fulfillment of an early twentieth-century avant-gardist dream, linear narrative is no longer the monolithic power in mass communication (though the promise of a satisfying narrative often remains the promotional "hook" with which to capture the consumer).

Instead, montage reigns as the vital aesthetic feature of American popular culture. The epistemological style of montage, which emphasizes arousal over all other human responses, has proliferated to the point of seeming organic, creating whole generations of sensibilities refined in its bouncy, colorful shadows. Media and genres that are hostile to montage speed—the all-print novel, the formal oral debate, the deduction-based whodunnit film—fall to the margins of popularity, voted down by the cultural democracy.

By contrast, the comic book has prospered in this environment, ascending to the status of the "graphic novel" in the minds of the timid few who remain too embarrassed to read comic books. The previously despised genre produced its first Pulitzer Prize winner in 1992: Art Spiegelman's *Maus*, an intimate penetration into the psychic horrors of the Holocaust. The visual style crafted by Steven Speilberg in *Schindler's List* (1993) owes much to Spiegelman's peculiar synthesis of orderly, matter-of-fact realism and chaotic, mind-dissembling phantasm. In a sense the film vulgarized the comic book's intricate style for the sake of mass consumption.

Television, which is both a cause and an effect of this historic movement toward montage, is despised for embodying the change by partisans of the culture of accreting narrative logics. But modifying or suppressing the free proliferation of television, as advocated by critics including Neil Postman and Gerry Mander, is not likely to reverse this profound aesthetic shift. Video games have already elevated traditional television genres into didactic, even pedagogical art forms.

An episode of *Nova* may not contain as much information as a given book on the same subject, but when it comes to learning about subtropical savannahs at eight o'clock in the evening on a Wednesday, many viewers are better prepared to absorb a modicum of data from the program's seamless audiovisual editing of facts and ideas than from blocks of printed text. *Oprah* and *Donahue* may not allow their guests to speak long enough to develop what might pass muster as an effective argument in a high school speech class, but many viewers are better prepared to be made aware of the pros and cons of condom distribution in high schools by talk shows that have chopped discourse into slivers of conversation. A copshow such as Stephen J. Cannell's *Silk Stalkings* (CBS/USA, 1991 to present) may not stimulate an appreciation of the post-industrial existential dilemma that gives intellectual dimension to Humphrey Bogart's grimaces in a Sam Spade movie, but many viewers are better prepared to swallow their dose of crime-and-punishment reaffirmation when it is diluted in the show's short-attention-span displays of beefcake and cheesecake strutting the screen in Sunbelt pastels.[2]

The model of social order that the dominance of montage has helped to create has proved excellent for cultivating credit-based consumption habits. Appetite is perpetually whetted by the flashing parade of images; satisfaction is relentlessly guaranteed. Self-realization through material comfort is marketed as, simultaneously, both utopian *and* attainable at reasonable terms. But this cradle-to-grave matrix of stimulus-response behavior has not proved so good for cultivating discipline-based production habits. Where Everyone is a King for whose delectation the wonders of the world are presented, not Everyone feels much like punching a clock. The positive relationship between pain and gain has migrated from the workplace of Puritan idealism to the health spa of hedonistic desire.

The inexorable commitment—the work—required of print to penetrate abstract symbols in order to get to the promised emotional and intellectual pleasures of *zee text* dooms reading to the status of an aesthetically spare activity gone begging in a lavish multimedia environment. Television viewing makes reading seem stoic and reading makes television viewing seem like relief. The TV viewer is invited to become a kind of just-fed Roman laying on a divan in the vomitorium, crying "Gimmee, gimmee," scanning the cable spectrum, voting life or death to every image with the imperial finger. In deep contrast, the spartan book says stop what you are doing and penetrate me; my rewards are buried inside.

Veteran TV viewers with thousands of hours of experience—child hedonists barely on the verge of discovering the organic depths of their own lust and greed—are sent to school to become readers, and the enormity of this task of transformation has left the educational system paralyzed. A vague debate gives form to the confusion. One side wants to fight the visceral allure of electronically generated montage in the name of linear, reason-based logics, arguing that such a revival might lead to higher SAT scores and, presumably, greater numbers of high school graduates who can read, write, and make correct change. In primary and secondary education this philosophy manifests itself in the "back to basics" movement, in higher education as the "great books" idea. Preparation for print culture participation is seen as a prerequisite to personal development, an immutable template of understanding essential for processing all information, including the high-tech data that seems to be eclipsing it.

The other side in this debate hopes to join rather than lick television, promoting an optimistic vision of the medium's attractive qualities integrated into the service of valued (or at least recognizable) intellectual traditions: erudite curiosity, historical consciousness, critical facility. This kind of thinking has yielded *Sesame Street,* cable-in-the-classroom, and teachers, well known at their schools, who show a lot of videotapes. Its advocates include political progressives who see yet again an extraordinary opportunity to spread the gospel of culture beyond the traditional class confines of literacy, as well as technological determinists who are convinced of the futility of swimming against the electronic current.

Little attention, however, is given to the possibility that neither strategy may map a plausible path back through contemporary communication circuitry to the real or imagined sacred ground of the literate mind, and that children are quite possibly being driven to further distraction by the mixed signals that result from this squabble among adults. Even as they learn from TV to watch TV or else risk becoming unhappy, alienated and hopelessly out-of-touch, kids get the message in no less certain terms that they ought to *stop* watching TV or else risk failing at the very tasks they must master to get the things that TV has promised will bring them fulfillment or relief from anxiety.

In their youthful exuberance some adolescent viewers have apparently transcended the confusion of this riddle by granting themselves license to kill people and take their money, sneakers, cars, or credit cards. Others—the future leaders of America—have succeeded in compartmentalizing and contextualizing the sensations of montage stimulation offered by their numerous home media appliances with the lessons of cause-and-effect logic offered in their schools. Able to appreciate the particulars of both the living room of perpetual arousal and the classroom of linear analysis, they inherit the protections of the law and become the rightful heirs to middle-class civilization: advertising agents, marketing analysts, public relations directors, lawyers, doctors, software *auteurs,* teachers, refrigeration maintenance engineers, and so on. And, as has always been the case, some of them will be damned good at it, too.

Unfortunately, not everybody can accomplish the key mental balancing act necessary for late twentieth-century legitimacy. For many viewers schooling in literacy is not much more than a pretense used to lend contour to the social activities of being brought up in America. According to a 1993 Federal Department of Education study administered by the Educational Testing Service (that's the SAT-GRE-LSAT-MCAT, etc. mafia), "Twenty-five percent of high school seniors across the country can barely read their diplomas."[3] Which is most significant? That they can't read the diplomas? That the diplomas were awarded to them despite the fact that they can't read them? Or that it took a tax-supported survey in order for professional educators to find this out? Perhaps none of the revelations of this study is half as striking as the conclusion drawn by Tom Ewing of the ETS concerning the 26,000 participants in the test sample: "The people who were surveyed had this misperception that they could read and write effectively. They would not define themselves as illiterate. But their perceptions didn't match the realities of the situation."[4]

Over 6,000 of those tested—and this was not a student group, but a cross-section of the American adult population—were unable to locate the expiration date on their driver's licenses. This seems more or less in concert with the familiar semi-monthly reports that flash through the daily news loops on CNN, all-news radio and the papers concerning schoolchildren who can't find Afghanistan or Kansas City on a map. Is it fair to speculate that if literacy was not so utterly remote from the requirements of everyday life in late twentieth-century America that many in the test group might have noticed the consequences of their reading deficiencies on their own? Is it fair to speculate that ruling elites will be recruited from among those who can read their high school diplomas and find the expiration dates on their driver's licenses as well as Afghanistan and Kansas City on a map? Will there be (is there already?) animosity, hostility, or violence between a multimedia communications elite holding the passwords to the databanks and a communications proletariat unable to crash through the spotless glass ceiling of subliteracy? Somewhere a child is booting up the brand-new PC that came with a birthday card. Somewhere else, close by, a clerk in a convenience store is wondering, "Maybe you know like I should try like to get into something with like computers or something?"

The Futility of Television Criticism

In the late 1970s I gave up writing about literature for writing about television. I made this career choice based on several reasons. The laziest was that it required less reading. The most ambitious was that the health of American culture and indeed the entire Western humanities tradition seemed to depend on somebody doing this dirty job. Some twenty years later, I find myself stuck in the curious position of writing (a medium of expression increasingly associated in the minds of most people with the stresses of a middle-class job requiring advanced schooling) about television (a medium of expression usually associated with the alleviation of stress by means of titillation). To read about television is to cancel out the advantages of both.

To give you an idea of how awkward a thing it is to try to write about television, the original editor of this book would not allow me to include in it any actual TV criticism (i.e., writing about programs or genres or performers or producers) because she believed that anyone who would buy a book about television, especially one with no pictures of stars in it, couldn't possibly be interested in—or even know what is being talking about—in essays concerning *The Flintstones, Green Acres,* Sid Caesar, Paddy Chayefsky, *Naked City,* or the other things I usually write about. It used to be that Manhattan publishing executives claimed not to have television sets. Now they admit to watching *Masterpiece Theater* and the news; the defense line of gentility shifts to not getting cable or maybe, by now, to not getting the premium channels.

Similarly, the editor of the former TV section, now "media" section, of *The Village Voice* stopped running my stuff because he found it too "literary" for the neobourgeois owners of home entertainment centers whom he imagines to be the demographic target of his brilliantly edited section. The blackboard Marxists who run the "left-wing" academic journals consider anything written on TV that doesn't contain a rote denouncement of laissez-faire capitalism—and its chief brainwashing tool, American TV—to be collaborationist. At the same time, the blackboard entrepreneurs who run the "right-wing" journals consider anything written on TV that doesn't contain a rote denouncement of bicoastal sitcom socialism to be politically (in)correct poppycock. This may provide a clue as to why *Entertainment Weekly* (print) and *Entertainment Tonight* (TV) provide the standard by which useful television criticism can be measured in the United States.

Every time I complain about the dilemma of trying to write *about* television, a relative asks me why I don't just chuck the whole criticism thing and try to write *for* television. Can anyone really believe that it's so easy to make a million dollars? Those people are geniuses. A person would have a better shot at getting rich by calling an 800 number, credit card handy, to order a six-pack of cassette tapes explaining the secrets of making a fortune by buying up mortgages from defunct savings and loans.

Actually the real reason I have been unable to save myself from a crime-terrorized future during which I am likely to become dependent upon the direct deposit of my Social Security check is that every single TV executive I've ever come in contact with has been so utterly sleazy—and has demonstrated that sleaziness so forthrightly, unashamedly and even arrogantly, almost as a form of greeting—so as to frighten me shitless. The TV industry may in fact be full of wonderfully creative folks possessing the remarkable talents necessary to bring laughter, tears, and information to the great multitudes of their fellow citizens. But so far I haven't bumped into any of that crowd, only dangerous gangsters who you wouldn't want to meet in a dark corridor of power.

And so my career as a television critic, born during the shank of the Network Era in an idealistic and innocent passion to describe the marvel of an emerging national drama in American culture, disintegrates along with the vision of a public role for criticism in a democratic culture. The dog-eared manifestos of my youth—*Democratic Vistas* by Walt Whitman and *The Public Arts* by Gilbert Seldes—share dusty shelf space with the works of Karl Marx, Marky Mark, Henry George, and Boy George, as I sit here with cable, VCR, computer game, and sadness in this queer West Hollywood ghetto, an only-too-human guinea pig for psychiatrists whose job it is to test out new regimens of antidepressive drugs (watch out for Paxil™—it pushed me from merely miserable to completely dysfunctional in less than three weeks, though I have a friend who has done quite well on it).

I stay up all night channel surfing, scanning for an infotaining info-mercial that will hold my attention long enough to at last make clear the essence of this quintessentially postmodern telegenre so that I might dream up an article on it for *The Atlantic* or *The Reader's Digest*. But where is my strength? Unable to withstand the psychic onslaught of even the first burst of brainless enthusiasm from the deliriously infotained consumers of the infomertional studio audience, I change the channel in less than a minute. Whereas once I prided myself on diving into the video muck, writing with energy, innocence, and imagined *je-ne-sais-crois* about professional wrestling, *The Beverly Hillbillies, Andy of Mayberry,* and the divinely inspired ethno-political theology espoused by Herbert W. Armstrong on *The World Tomorrow,* now I am so grossed out by *Geraldo* that I change the channel in less than a minute, hardly enough time enough for Sally Jesse or anyone else to convince me that my father sodomized me. Oh, Mnemosyne, why have you deserted me? Some days CNN is so painful that my Walter Lippman-like rage to see narrative order imposed upon the chaos of the world is outstripped by the mystical negative brain-death vibes that even a middle-level news day can generate. Who cries tears for Bosnia as camera bleeds to sports highlights? I turn on *Crossfire* but change the channel in less than a minute. Even if the collapse of Soviet Communism has left Islamic fundamentalism as the only serious countervailing force to world capitalism, I somehow still cling to a belief that the spectrum of critical thinking on the condition of the human race is not defined in any satisfying boundaries by the incestuous cross-kvetching of Michael Kinsley, Fred Barnes, John McLaughlin, Eleanor Clift, and Patrick Buchanan, no matter how many shows, channels, and cable networks they appear on separately, in pairs, or ensemble during any given broadcast day. Did Michael Kinsley ever actually say, "I'm not a liberal, but I play one on TV," or is that just a joke that went around? Is John McLaughlin in line to be the second General Electric spokesperson to occupy the White House? Doesn't Fred Barnes look like the guy who used to play the father in *Dennis the Menace?* See Segment Four for a snide remark on Patrick Buchanan. Here's a critical judgment for you: Robert Novak has descended into baroque reasonableness since his forced departure from *The McLaughlin Group.*

I like *The Simpsons* (it's humane), *Beavis and Butthead* (social realism), and *Law and Order* (it reminds me of literature). I like *L. A. Law* and *NYPD Blue* because the dialogue and plot construction in Steven Bochco productions are generally better than you're likely to find with a twenty-five dollar theater ticket, and the only price you have to pay is watching the commercials. Some television critic I turned out to be.

So as not to paint an unduly negative portrait of the television critic as a not-so-young-anymore unipolar depressive, I ought to mention that there was what could be described as a high point in my late great career. It came in the spring of 1989, a quasi-pathetic bob in the tumultuous wake of the Reagan presidency. That April, America celebrated the fiftieth anniversary of its first broadcast of a television signal to the public and because I was apparently the only person teaching at a major accredited college in the United States unconcerned enough about my personal status to acknowledge it, I found myself on the clock for a Warhol quarter hour.

That was some year. I appeared on *60 Minutes* and shot the shit with a set of carefully constructed Morley Safer reaction shots. If gossip will help sales of this book I don't mind *revealing* that the saintly Morley chainsmoked Rothman's cigarettes every second the camera wasn't on him and that he even brandished a hip flask at carefully selected moments though I cannot account for its contents. The interview lasted over two hours and, not surprisingly, my best one-liner didn't make it to the couple of minutes that actually got used on the air. I take you, by means

of print, to the cutting room floor (I must paraphrase because CBS owns
the documentation and will not release it to me):

> *Morley:* I've been in the TV business since it started and I know all
> kinds of producers and executives and most of them tell me that most
> of the time people hardly even pay attention to their TV sets. So what
> purpose is there to spending all this time analyzing television programs?
>
> *David:* People hardly pay attention? Do you think that's what CBS tells
> Procter and Gamble when they charge them a quarter of a million
> dollars for a twenty-second spot?

I was a guest on *The Today Show* and had the experience of being
interviewed by Bryant Gumbel whose remarkable talent, I learned while
appearing on live national television at seven in the morning (awakened
at five!), is an uncanny ability to jump in and change the subject during
the split second necessary for humans to draw breath while speaking.
Back on tape, Bernard Goldberg interviewed me for a piece that appeared
on *The CBS Evening News with Dan Rather.* He used me on the air for
about ten seconds, but in his narration of the piece, he quoted liberally
from my writing, failing to attribute the source. In fact, at times it sort
of sounded like he had written the words. The following day I called him
up and asked him why he didn't at least credit me for a direct quotation
from my book. He told me I lived in an "ivory tower" and that he lived
in the "real world." I suppose that's true. In the ivory tower we call that
"plagiarism"; what do you call it in the real world?

I also wrote an essay for the lifestyle section of *The Philadelphia
Inquirer* concerning the invention of television. I was hoping to open up
a new career "front": daily newspapers. I imagined myself writing the
first paragraphs of this article in the speaking voice of Walter Winchell:

> 1927 was a momentous year for popular American success stories.
> Lucky Lindy flew The Spirit of St. Louis across the Atlantic; the Babe
> slammed sixty homers for the New York Yankees; and Al Jolson told a
> disbelieving audience, "You ain't heard nothing yet," in the first talking
> picture. But that same year, a young inventor named Philo T. Farns-
> worth from the Mormon farming town of Rigby, Idaho—working in a
> modest laboratory with data he had collected in his own high school
> science notebooks—would pull a stunt that would in some ways top
> them all. Demonstrating a remarkable new invention that he had
> dubbed the "image dissector," Farnsworth, who had lived the first four-
> teen years of his life in a house without electricity, electronically trans-

mitted a picture from one end of the lab to the other. The show, lasting less than a minute, consisted of a fuzzy though prophetic image glowing on a tiny screen: a U.S. dollar sign!

By 1930, Farnsworth had refined his system to the brink of commercial viability. The Philadelphia Storage Battery Company (also known as Philco) learned of this real-life Tom Swift and brought him east to a state-of-the-art research and development lab on the banks of the Schuylkill River. Meanwhile, over in Princeton, New Jersey, Philco's giant rival, the Radio Corporation of America, was involved in research of its own concerning the tantalizing possibilities of "radio with pictures." Vladimir Zworykin, the Russian emigrant scientist who headed the company's team, patented his version of the device, calling it the "iconoscope." By the end of the 1930s, RCA would be ready to begin regular television transmission to the public—but not before losing an expensive patent infringement case to the backyard inventor from Idaho.

Philco did go into the business of manufacturing television sets for a time, but the company would always be better known for its radios, eventually becoming the audio division of the Ford Motor Company. RCA, on the other hand, anxious to sell its television receivers to the public, went directly into business of TV broadcasting. Through its subsidiary NBC, the company set up studios at the New York World's Fair in a pavilion shaped like a giant radio tube. RCA made its—and the world's—first formal telecast to the American people on April 30, 1939, featuring opening day ceremonies at the fair. Following David Sarnoff's introduction of the medium, Franklin D. Roosevelt gave the ribbon-cutting speech, thus becoming the first U.S. president to appear on television.

By September 1940, WNBT, the world's first bonafide commercial TV station, was offering daily service to the approximately 10,000 television sets that were believed to exist in the New York metropolitan area (many of them belonged to RCA employees and their relatives). Pioneer couch potatoes were treated to what now seems like a rather spare diet of newsreels, puppet shows, travelogues, cartoons, variety shows, and even rumba lessons. There was a cooking show, but the menu was limited to salads because the studio lights were so hot that engineers feared the consequences of turning on the oven. On July 1, 1941, having gained FCC approval, WNBT began selling commercial time; any advertiser fool enough to spend the money could sponsor an hour of prime-time TV for the grand sum of $120.

World War II put a damper on a lot of things, and television was one of them. The government decreed that optical sitcoms and quiz shows would have to wait for a while as the nation shifted its wartime research aims to such unentertaining projects as radar development and the atom bomb. TV went back on the air, however, soon after the war's end. The three largest national radio networks—NBC, CBS and ABC —all formed television networks out of the stations that began to spring up around the country. (A fourth network, DuMont, was attempted by television manufacturer Allen B. DuMont, but it went dark in 1955.)

Wrestling, roller derby, and amateur talent contests went over big on the new medium, as did the acts of former vaudevillians such as Milton Berle and Red Skelton. Popular radio sitcoms such as *Burns and Allen, The Jack Benny Program, Amos 'n Andy,* and *The Goldbergs* switched overnight to TV production. Though NASA had yet to send a missile into space, Brooklyn bus driver Ralph Kramden was making weekly offers to his wife Alice of trips to the moon. A Philadelphia disc jockey named Dick Clark even managed to attract a national audience by training a camera on a bunch of local teenagers dancing to rock and roll music in the middle of the afternoon.

Though hampered a bit by technical problems and by a freeze on new stations during the Korean War, television's penetration into every nook and cranny of the American continent and consciousness was remarkably swift and thorough. In 1950, only five years after the Japanese had surrendered to MacArthur, there were already one million American homes that had become, in the industry's jargon, "HUTs" (or "Households Using TV"). By the time John Kennedy's boyish grin stood up to challenge Richard Nixon's five o'clock shadow in the first nationally televised presidential election debate in 1960, there were almost 600 TV stations in the United States sending out their signals to no less than 50 million sets.

As the commercial stakes spiraled in prime-time advertising, the early sense of playfulness and experimentation that could be found in the work of the TV pioneers—in the comedy of Ernie Kovacs and Sid Caesar, the drama of Rod Serling and Paddy Chayefsky, the dynamic news reporting of Edward R. Murrow—gradually fell victim to the quality control managers who preferred the safe bets of formula sit-coms, copshows and Ken-and-Barbie newscasts. With a cozy group of a dozen or so production companies supplying virtually all programming to a market consisting of three corporate buyers, blandness and uniformity became the foremost qualities associated with the medium. In a few of the larger cities, some variety was offered to the viewer by what was then known as "educational TV." But the Public Broadcasting Service (PBS) would not be exposing the American public to British *Kultur* or the private lives of kangaroos on a full-scale basis until 1969.

For all its problems, American television emerged as a truly extraordinary historical phenomenon: a medium of communication that reached across the traditional cultural boundaries of class, region, race, and ethnicity to supply an eclectic pluralistic nation-state with what amounted to a national drama. The sheer force of TV was spectacularly pervasive. Who didn't know who Lucy was? Or Walter Cronkite? Or the Fonz? Who could fail to recognize the ominous "dummm-dee-dum-dum" of *Dragnet?* And of course everyone would catch the Great Communicator's act. Americans who grew up during the oligopoly of CBS, NBC, and ABC could not help but believe that this single national three-ring circus would last forever. As the television industry reaches the half-century mark, however, it is handing itself over to yet another technological innovation and that, of course, is cable.

With most of the households in the United States now wired for cable, the Big Three's average collective share of the prime-time audience has diminished from over 90 percent to under 60 percent of viewers, and that percentage is bound to fall even further as the cable continues to snake its way down the American boulevard. As a result, broadcasting gradually gives way to "narrowcasting."

Whereas once a family might have sat around the living room TV set—McLuhan's "electronic hearth"—gathered together to watch an episode of *All in the Family* or *Little House on the Prairie* or *The Bionic Woman*, nowadays Dad is just as likely to slip off to the den to look at the ball game on ESPN, while Mom enjoys an episode of *Cagney and Lacey* on Lifetime, as Junior tunes in USA Network to catch the Hulkster's latest comeback and Sis rocks out with MTV. With so many channels slicing up the national audience into ever-tinier slivers, the center will not hold. The great "mass" audience of network television is being picked apart into the target "class" audiences of cable TV.

The first decades of American television are likely to be remembered as that quaint period during which virtually the whole nation was watching the same tiny menu of TV programs, just as the current-day cable subscriber is amused by the image of a single TV transmitter beaming out a signal to a few privileged set owners in 1939. As technology continues to develop, television transcends the entertainment and information functions its inventors had imagined. Americans are already shopping, worshipping God, and taking diplomas with their TV sets. What's next? A chess game with a pal on the other side of town— or in Russia? Medical help beaming across the screen in response to an emergency call? How about voting? All these things are now technologically feasible.

Fifty years ago, no less literate an observer of the American scene than E. B. White attended that first public demonstration of TV at the New York World's Fair. He was moved to write, "I believe television is going to be the test of the modern world, and that in this new opportunity to see beyond the range of our vision, we shall discover a new and unbearable disturbance of the modern peace, or a saving radiance in the sky. We shall stand or fall by television—of that I am quite sure."[5]

A Religious Experience

The radio companies that researched, developed, and marketed television weren't much interested in the technological messianism expressed by E. B. White or other visionary critics. "We're in the same position of a plumber laying a pipe," NBC boss David Sarnoff told *Fortune* magazine in 1958. "We're not responsible for what goes through the pipe."[6] Leonard Goldenson, Sarnoff's counterpart at ABC, got even hotter under the collar when confronted with the notion that TV might be a determiner, as opposed to merely a conduit, of culture. "Can we legislate taste?" he asked an FCC committee. "Shall we set up a *commissar* of culture?"[7] Tough talk at a time when *Bolsheviki* still held the Kremlin and were widely thought to have designs on the White House.

It seemed clear to the boardroom boys that the bonanza they had made in radio advertising could be duplicated and topped with TV. They defined their job as the selling of sets to the public and commercials to the corporations, refusing to acknowledge that they were also peddling a structure of social organization—a culture—to society. That just turned out to be the Crackerjack that came along with the prize in the box.

A half-century later it hardly needs to be argued that television viewing is a fundamental form of social organization in America, intimately related by measures of competition and collaboration with such primary communal structures as blood-based nuclear family, workplace cohort, street gang, and religious affiliation. Some commentators, notably right-wing clerics such as Reverend Donald E. Wildmon and Reverend Jerry Falwell, blame television content—especially representations of sex and violence—for the stunning crack-up of the family, and of civil order in general, that has occurred during the years since TV became a household appliance. The limitation of the fundamentalist critique is that like its counterpart, leftwing neo-Puritanism, it is utterly content-based.

In the case of televangelists, not only do they fail to question, probe, or challenge the formal consequences of keeping a TV set active in the home, but most of them shamelessly seek to capitalize on its presence, aligning themselves, by means of their 800 numbers and "partnership" offers, to the ubiquitous commercialism that the medium has brought to even the most intimate corners of domestic life. Embracing the technological fiat of television, they profess a faith that they can control the ramifications of mass socialization to viewing by popularizing their own software, exchanging what they view as Madison Avenue and Hollywood's post-Darwinian secular humanist programming for something more amenable to that old time religion.

Though wildly overstating the case in terms of the modernist credentials that he bestows upon network television, Pat Robertson put it this way in a 1979 interview:

> We need to get into the arts and the media. I mean the church, after all, dominated the theater and music and art for centuries, and we've just totally given it up. We've given it up to nihilism. The art that comes out is nihilistic. Sartre, Camus, these people, they have no hope, nothing, and the art reflects that. . . . I'd like to see us get into all of this; that's the kingdom.[8]

The founding elder of the Christian Broadcasting Network and host of *The 700 Club*, Robertson has battled the influence of post-war French existentialism upon his coast-to-coast and worldwide congregation with an eclectic arsenal of video bludgeons: *Father Knows Best* and *Bonanza* reruns, Bible-based cartoons, Christ-centered cooking shows and his own daily Republican Party talk-variety hour. Though regular viewers are still occasionally asked to hit their knees screenside and pray with the host for spontaneous remission of life-threatening diseases, or improvement of the GNP or other such favors, the rougher pre-Darwinist edges of CBN seem to be smoothing out. In 1988, for example, the Christian Broadcasting Network changed its name to The Family Channel, shifting promotional emphasis from religious to social function. Similarly, CBN University, as exquisitely postmodern a name for a school as was ever chiseled in a cornerstone, was rechristened Regent University, a name betraying more than a little bit of ivy envy. Robertson, himself a Yale man, is rarely seen these days appealing directly to the Lord to divert hurricanes away from his satellite ground station; he is more likely to be calmly explaining Biblical injunctions against national health insurance.

Does TV have an inevitable cooling effect on the transmission of fire and brimstone? Is the temptation to gain audience share so great that any ideologically committed mass communication venture will inevitably regulate its own radicalism by means of an interior management argument between those who want to reach out to make new converts—stretching doctrine where necessary—and those who see the reaching out as selling out?

The discussion among the braintrust at CBN in the mid-1980s is not difficult to imagine: Let's drop "Christian" from the logo; we'll bring in the doubting Thomases. What? Are we ashamed to be Christians? Of course not, but what's in a name; a rose by any other . . . And so the technologically determined paradigmatic debate divides, conquers, and absorbs yet another potential radical critique into a mainstreamed culture-niche option. "Concern with *effect* rather than *meaning*," McLuhan points out in *Understanding Media*, "is a basic change of our electric time, for effect involves the total situation and not a single level of information movement."[9]

The refusal of the Teleright to oppose television as a hardware—the refusal to tell people, from the pulpit, to get that blaspheming thing out of their homes or else—is defensively justified on the air by the argument that it is only through TV that the Biblical injunction to preach the gospel to every corner and creature on the face of the earth can be fulfilled. That being the case, it is only natural that the Devil would have a particularly passionate interest in infesting the potentially sacred medium with Godless pornography, a wide category that includes everything from *Married . . . With Children* to "left-liberal" biases on network news stories. Thus, as the second millennium draws to a close, the war between the forces of light and darkness is defined by Christian broadcasters as a series of battles over the appropriateness of TV programming rather than over the appropriateness of TV, which is the issue that continues to preoccupy the debate within the secular humanist educational establishment.

The software counteroffensive of the Christian Right extends far beyond television: Christian rock, Christian radio, Christian computer games, Christian stand-up comedy, Christian greeting cards, even Christian bookstores. The secular-humanist trollop will be challenged by Our Lady of Pop Culture on every street corner. A Third Great Awakening, Christian Pop began as a direct reaction to the breakdown of Victorian standards in American mainstream popular culture, which is the chief enduring legacy of the 1960s. While some old-school ministries have reacted to mainstream pop culture's post-1960s indifference toward Christian propriety by organizing old-fashioned camp-meeting bonfire burnings of records, cassettes, CDs, and videotapes (books, though better kindling than plastic or metal, are hardly worth the trouble at this point), the more savvy ministries have eschewed this "hot" negativity, which plays so poorly on TV. Instead, they coolly build their own media empires, attempting to beat the demon at his own game.

For a practical illustration of the "dueling softwares" phenomenon at work in the demographically pluralized cable environment, try switching back and forth for a few minutes between a PBS affiliate and a Christian broadcasting station. With some skill at remote-control finger editing and a bit of luck you may be able to momentarily deny, say, a Professor Carl Sagan and a Reverend James Robison the demographic safeties they enjoy while preaching to the converted from their home pulpits, and to put them instead into a more meaningful split-screen dialogue. This creates an extraordinary opportunity to judge whether, as William Jennings Bryan put it earlier this century, "It is better for one to trust in the Rock of Ages than in the age of rocks; it is better for one to know that he is close to the Heavenly Father, than to know how far the stars in the heavens are apart." [10]

According to the A. C. Nielsen Company, most televiewing takes place in the central commercial zone of a continuum whose left and right epistemological borders may be drawn at PBS television and Christian broadcasting. But because TV is itself a quintessential product of secular humanist empiricism, or perhaps because I am, science seems to come out looking more telegenic than spirit does on a video screen. The larger commercial enterprise, of which most Christian broadcasters (as well as public television stations) have made themselves a part, sells things—material objects—on the promise and premise that these items will make life on this earth happier and more fulfilling. Redemption can be imagined as a state of grace, but it must be sold as a tangible product. J. Walter Thompson recognized this during the 1920s radio advertising boom when he described Jesus Christ as the first advertising man. Though full of all kinds of shopping tips, TV offers little advice on the subject of eternity. The soul is simply not as camera-friendly as the flesh.

In his essay "Television and Moral Order in a Secular Age," Victor Lidz writes

> Television . . . has been aligned mainly with the claims of the secular order. The network audience during prime time is addressed in terms provided almost entirely by the secular culture. The God who is occasionally invoked is the curiously abstract figure conceived as a foundation of the "entire Judeo-Christian tradition" in the now conventional phrase. He is called upon through a precise etiquette only to frame a statement of moral commitment and underscore the good faith with which it is intended. The overt action of prime-time, network television is enclosed within worldly concerns that focus on job, family, health, safety, neighborhood, law-and-order, skill, achievements, material well being, success, fellowship, and loyalty to nation and way-of-life. . . . Life is depicted as largely enclosed within the realities of the secular order, as even comprehensible only within its prosaic terms.[11]

Though dutifully revered in commercial genres when He comes up in conversation, God on TV is ultimately relegated to the dubious status of a print power, a legendary figure who, in a pre-laser beam techno-environment, blasted the characters of the Ten Commandments out of

stone, who revealed His will to the People of the Book in the Old Testa-
ment, who sent His only begotten Son to inspire the accounts of divine
intervention that were collected for print distribution in the New Testa-
ment.[12] It is with Book in hand, not Watchman or Newton, that Jimmy
Swaggart warns viewers of the consequences of committing the sins that
he has committed. The Book is honored, perhaps more ceremoniously
than ever before. But is it the object of wonderment? Is it loved or feared?

Clerics interested in the future of their religions might do better to
ponder the salient differences that divide an audience that is slouching
on couches, clutching at joysticks, and fingering remote control units,
from a congregation sitting upright in the pews holding their prayer
books in their palms. Arguments over specific depictions of sex, violence,
Halloween paganism, sexual orientation, or any other particular types of
dramatic plot content on television may only be giving publicity—and at
this moment that probably means comfort—to the Devil.[13]

Television has already played a definitive role in the migration of
drama—both fiction-based and news-based—from sacred or elevated
space (i.e., church or theater) to profane or low milieus (den . . . bed-
room . . . plastic bus station waiting room seat . . . toilet and so on). This
relocation of aesthetic experience from exalted public places to intimate,
isolated private sites has been a technologically driven process that has
taken place in leaps over several centuries. The introduction to the home
of newspapers, magazines, affordable books, and radio have all contrib-
uted to it, dangling the teats of externally manufactured consciousness
into domestic life. But the shift of professionally produced cultural activity from ritualized community settings to the places where people eat
and excrete has been made fait accompli by television. If once imaginable
as a refuge from the world of commerce, politics and social discomforts,
the home now becomes the chief landing point for the endless invasion
of the messages. By Victorian standards, it is hardly a fit place any more
for a family to live.

Especially since the Enlightenment, a variety of Western atheists,
agnostics, deists, and political radicals have questioned whether Christianity is primarily a religion, in the sense of a way to know God, to
worship God, and to gain spiritual redemption from God, or whether it
is primarily a form of social organization that has allowed the rich to get
richer and the poor to have children in some kind of an orderly manner.
Like Christianity and most other religions, TV offers its congregants
a coherent story concerning how to live in the world. It provides its
attendees with a steady stream of allegories, suggestions, and didactic
pep talks on the subjects of success and how to achieve it under a set of
rules.

Televangelists make a mistake when they call secular humanism a religion and castigate the networks for presenting programming that is infused with its theology. Emile Zola and Clarence Darrow would be just as disappointed by the bill of fare in the *TV Guide* as Cardinal Newman and William Jennings Bryan. J. Walter Thompson and Darren Stevens, on the other hand, might be quite pleased. Television is the oracle of a religion called consumerism and as such it does not lend itself easily to use as a transmission medium for one or more other religions that hold conflicting accounts of the past and the future or that challenge its basic tenet of personal empowerment and salvation through dedication to consumption as lifelong practice.

Opponents of consumerism—right, left and otherwise—are generally blind to the nature of consumerism's dominance. To secular humanists network TV is another dangerous drug served up by the dealers who gave you the opium of the masses; to born-again Christians it is another false messiah brought to you by the folks who gave you Darwin, Freud, and Marx. But consumerism is a revolution against the paradigm used by both sides to explain consumerism. The messiah has both arrived and is arriving at all times. Utopia is both declared and imminent. The commercial has made the material spiritual. There's no use complaining about the shortcomings of life, except that complaining reminds you that you are looking for solutions. Remedies are available. Buy them.

I Quit

When I took up television criticism as a vocation in the late 1970s I did not see myself as a divinity student pursuing the theology of consumerism. Go ahead, call me a remnant of the synthesis of secular and religious cultural idealisms that took place among the Ashkenazic Jews who immigrated to New York City before the First World War. Call me that or call me *pisher*. But I had actually thought that by writing about television I would be bearing witness to a significant historical event: a democratization of culture being carried out by technological means. After all, broadcasting had removed the final logistical obstacle to the distribution of a body of information, drama, music, and the other arts to all classes of society—a signal so strong that it penetrated the very monolith of illiteracy. For anybody holding faith in the improving capacities of the humanities, what more exciting event could occur in the annals of civilization than the invention of a means to make plentiful to the mind what had always been the scarce sources of aesthetic nutrition?

But go figure. Instead of achieving full distribution of the wealth of culture, television has developed in such a way as to beg a series of extremely disturbing questions that are so threatening to the nobler currents of humanistic thinking that they are rarely discussed, not even on talk shows or at academic conferences. Is it possible that many or most people are unprepared for the needle-shower of imaginative stimulation rained upon them each day by their TV sets and their other household culture appliances? Is it possible that the democratic admission to the theater accomplished by television has filled the seats with audience members who cannot grasp the essential "play world-real world" concept, the very thing that makes drama a civilized activity? Has the blare of television merely disturbed the drowsy consciousness of a monster, like the blast of an atomic bomb dropped on a prehistoric egg in a 1950s Japanese sci-fi picture?

In the early nineteenth century, de Tocqueville's safari through America convinced him that the arts, as they had evolved in Europe, were not compatible with the social system that he saw developing in the trans-Atlantic wilderness.[14] In the European courts and churches, great concentrations of wealth and political power had created great concentrations of taste and aesthetic power. Democratic consensus, he allowed, might help bring about political balance and perhaps even a greater degree of economic evenhandedness. But the imagination, he concluded, would not flourish where equilibrium is sought through aesthetic compromise. Consensus must be challenged by the excellent display of the extreme and the extraordinary if art is to have a chance. Fastidiousness of appreciation, as the count called it, had to have sway over quantity of consumption.

Not so in the realm of A. C. Nielsen. Ever since culture became an industrial commodity sold by a producing elite to whomever could pay, there have been members of the consuming audience who are not even exactly quite sure of what they are buying. Any actor playing a villain on a soap opera is well aware that a walk in the park may at any moment be disturbed by an angry fan anxious to set him straight on the evils of philandering. When I worked at NBC, a colleague in the Audience Response Department would entertain us at lunch with letters from fans asking for driving instructions to fictional towns. Proposals of marriage for hot *dramatis personae* arrive at the networks by the mailbag.

Examples of this kind of thing are so common that they can be found in virtually any issue of a fan magazine or a weekly tabloid. (It is only when physical violence is involved that these items spiral into the grimmer rhythms of the daily news media.) This tidbit, for instance, appeared in *Entertainment Weekly;* it concerns the star of *NYPD Blue*, the "upmarket" Bochco cop show that premiered on ABC in 1993:

As David Caruso can attest . . . (his) . . . relationship . . . (to the audience) . . . can be very personal. "The other day I was working," he recounts, "and two . . . girls pull up in a car and they say . . . "You're makin' a mistake! Go back to your wife! That other girl, she's not right for you!" [15]

In his book *Television Culture*, John Fiske explores the phenomenon of art-life confusion among TV viewers by comparing it to an aficionado's appreciation of realism in high culture:

> In literature or highbrow drama, it is the mark of skill and art of the author to create such characters. . . . Bradley's (1904) work on Shakespeare's tragedies is often seen as the one that established and validated this tradition: in it he treats Shakespeare's heroes and heroines as if they were real people with independent lives outside the plays, and uses this psychological realism to prove Shakespeare's genius.
>
> When this confusion between a character and a real person occurs, however, in forms . . . such as soap opera, its effects are derided, not praised. The soap opera fans who fantasize characters into real people (sometimes to the extent of writing them letters) are derided for their stupidity while critics such as . . . Bradley are praised for their insight. In fact, the fans and . . . the dramatic critics both retain, even if in a suppressed form, the awareness of the difference between a character and a person: the illusion of realism is only as complete as we allow or wish it to be. [16]

Fiske's optimistic view that contemporary fans are merely engaging in a little turn-of-the-century avant-garde drama criticism when they write letters to people who they ought to know are only figments of other people's imaginations certainly applies to some or even most members of the TV audience. But that audience numbers in the tens, no hundreds, of millions. What about the others, even a "tiny" minority? What about the fans who have come to depend upon television as the oracle of *imago mundi*, as documentary *mimesis*, as a representation of "the real world" that cannot otherwise be known from where they sit?

How far a leap is it from failing to understanding the differences between (a) representational drama and (b) the rest of reality, to a belief that the upper middle-class style of life and point of view portrayed on that same little screen is the normal condition of humanity, and that to live beneath it is to live beneath dignity? How far a leap is it to the decision that it is better to live in violence than without dignity? Such has always been the credo of revolutionaries, including those you are likely to agree with and those you are likely to disagree with.

Do you think prostitution is humiliating? Do you think drug addiction is degrading? Do you think committing violence is a dehumanizing act? What about not having a car? Or a VCR? Or cable? What about lacking sneakers that command the respect of one's peers? New forms of personal debasement are manufacturing new forms of violence at assemblyline speed, making it increasingly difficult to be careful out there. The rhythm of television is a bland steady beat, the once exciting speed of montage made banal by repetition. The white-noisiness is occasionally interrupted by a pinprick of interest, and once in a greater while it is brought to crescendo by the rush of arousal: lust, envy, disgust, or some other powerful body response. If TV is too boring, it is only because it is too stimulating to develop any interest in.

A newsblip on *Beavis and Butthead* appeared in the fall of 1993, which may or may not be forgotten by the time you are reading this. A kid in Florida set his house on fire. His mother threatened all kinds of law suits, claiming that her son watched the show and heard Butthead say to Beavis, "Fire is cool," thus provoking arson. Predictably, anti-*Beavis and Butthead* forces identified themselves and began massing. The incident was discussed in Congress. As usually happens in such cases, the free speech issue was trotted out by the pro-*Beavis and Butthead* forces, making the whole thing too complicated by hiding the issue behind a "First Amendment smokescreen," which allowed the tempest to disappear into a teapot of confusion and indifference. The issue of the function of art in society was dismissed from the discussion by both sides on the dubious technicality that *Beavis and Butthead* doesn't qualify for such consideration: the antis adopt this line because they hate the show aesthetically; the pros, because they want to trivialize the show, which is helpful to their argument that too much power is being attributed to it.

But how does the case of a TV viewer setting a fire after watching a TV show differ from the case of, say, a late nineteenth-century middle-class reader reading *Madame Bovary,* finding empathy with the character, and deciding to go out and have a sexually fulfilling love affair at the expense of marriage vows and the social function of marriage in society? In at least one way it doesn't. In both cases—in all cases—art is dangerous (see Plato's *Republic*). The opening up of the Pandora's box of the human imagination is not the nerdy little recitation of a rhyming couplet that dominates bourgeois mythology via primary school lesson plans. Art, or anything rating that word, affects the consciousness of those who give themselves to the experience. Sometimes, having tested out an imagined experience through the human capacities for identification, empathy, and sympathy, people act, even act radically, in their own lives.

The problem with the *Beavis and Butthead* viewer may have been that he was completely overwhelmed by the impulses and feelings stimulated by aesthetic experience, that he had not received an education that had prepared him for *Beavis and Butthead*. He willingly suspended his disbelief without knowing that he was doing that—or even what that was—and the fire department had to be called in. His pleasure from the text overpowered his social instincts. Art stimulated him to shake up life and he did just that. As difficult as this is to accept for worshippers at the temple of secular humanism, such stimulation may not always have good results.

In the early days of electronic media, traditionalist conservatives were fond of the point that culture was a privilege, not a right, and that not all members of society had "earned" it. In *The Revolt of the Masses* (1932), José Ortega y Gasset observes "two classes of creatures" in society: those who have tastes, dreams, wishes, desires, and sensitivity; and "the multitude," a nameless, faceless crowd that can be stimulated and manipulated with icons and artifacts, but is incapable of the delicate balance of intellectual and visceral pleasure that make for aesthetic experience.[17]

Dozens of electronic media later, the stakes have been stretched, along with the definition of culture. If there are two classes of creatures in the information society they are those who are driven to the beta wave state by the messages, which they find relaxing, and those who are driven to distraction by the messages, which they find damning. In America, both groups are armed, but the latter group is hungrier to discharge its tension and that may be why the relaxed will have to be content to make themselves prisoners in their own home entertainment centers.

Are you, as a person reading a book, predisposed to see yourself and readers in general as above this conflict, or perhaps as the victims of it, but in no way responsible for the terror?

1. I don't mean to be obtuse when I write "Despite, or perhaps because of" here. I'm genuinely undecided. On the one hand, the popularity of reruns would seem to indicate that the audience is as obsessed as ever at watching naturalistic, cause-and-effect narrative drama; on the other hand, endless exposure and reexposure to these same narratives may have proved key in taking the blush off the narrative rose and thus had a causal effect on the ascendancy of montage.

2. It is worth mentioning that some college students complain about being assigned to watch black-and-white movies, in much the same tone that preceding generations complained about the length of assigned readings. As for silent movies, they are considered a form of torture comparable to reading a book the size and complexity of George Eliot's *Middlemarch*.

3. Elizabeth Mehren, "Test Scores Are Low, but What Do They Measure?" *Los Angeles Times,* 29 Sept. 1993, Sec. E1.

4. Ibid.

5. E. B. White, as quoted in "The First Image, A Dollar Sign," *Philadelphia Inquirer,* 2 May 1989.

6. As cited in William Boddy, *Fifties Television* 239.

7. Ibid.

8. As cited in Carol Flake, *Redemptorama: Culture, Politics and the New Evangelicism* (New York: Doubleday, 1984), 137.

9. H. Marshall McLuhan, *Understanding Media* (New York: Signet, 1964), 39.

10. As quoted in *Inherit the Wind* dir. Stanley Kramer (United Artists, 1960).

11. Victor Lidz, "Television and Moral Order in a Secular Age," in *Media in Society,* ed., Caren J. Deming and Samuel Becker, (Glenview, Ill.: Scott Foresman, 1988), 55–56.

12. Recent novels that have explored the impact of print's decline on Christianity include Gore Vidal's *Live from Golgotha* and Wilbert Barnhard's *Gospel.*

13. See chapter 3 for a discussion of Hans Magnus Enzensberger's treatment of this issue in *The Consciousness Industry.*

14. "In What Spirit the Americans Cultivate the Arts," *Democracy in America* (1835, reprinted in *Mass Culture: The Popular Arts in America,* ed. Bernard Rosenberg and David M. White (New York: Free Press, 1957), 27–34.

15. Lisa Schwarzbaum, "Top Cops," *Entertainment Weekly* 29 Oct. 1993, 21.

16. John Fiske, *Television Culture* (New York: Methuen, 1987), 153.

17. José Ortega y Gasset, "The Coming of the Masses," in *The Revolt of the Masses* (1932, reprinted in *Mass Culture: The Popular Arts in America* ed. Bernard Rosenberg and David M. White, (New York: Free Press, 1957), 43.

Bibliography
Index

Bibliography

Adorno, Theodor W. "Television and the Patterns of Mass Culture." *Quarterly of Film, Radio and Television* 8 (1954): 213.

Alter, Robert. *The Pleasures of Reading in an Ideological Age.* New York: Simon and Schuster, 1989.

Anders, Gunther. "The Phantom World of TV." Translated by Norbert Guterman. *Dissent* 3 (1956): 14.

Arnold, Matthew. *Culture and Anarchy.* Edited by J. Dover Wilson. 1869. Reprint, London: Cambridge Univ. Press, 1950.

Bayles, Martha. "Taking Sitcoms Seriously." *New York Times Sunday Book Review* 30 Apr. 1989.

Bloom, Allan. *The Closing of the American Mind.* New York: Simon and Schuster, 1987.

Boddy, William. *Fifties Television: The Industry and Its Critics.* Urbana: Univ. of Illinois Press, 1993.

Brooks, Tim, and Earle Marsh. *The Complete Directory to Prime-Time Network Television Programs.* 5th ed. New York: Ballantine, 1992.

Cady, Barbara, and Norman Lear. "Playboy Interview: Norman Lear." *Playboy* 23 (Mar. 1976): 53–69.

Cripps, Thomas. *"Amos 'n' Andy* and the Struggle for Racial Integration." In *American History/American Television,* edited by John E. O'Conner, 33–54. New York: Ungar 1983.

Czitrom, Daniel J. *Media and the American Mind.* Chapel Hill: Univ. of North Carolina Press, 1983.

DeLillo, Don. *White Noise.* New York: Penguin, 1985.

D'Souza, Dinesh. *Illiberal Education.* New York: Vintage, 1992.

Eco, Umberto. *Travels in Hyper Reality.* Translated by William Weaver. San Diego: Helen and Kurt Wolff/Harcourt Brace Jovanovich, 1986.

Eliot, T. S. "Notes Toward the Definition of Culture." In *Christianity and Culture,* 79–202. New York: Harcourt, 1968.

Emerson, Ralph Waldo. "The American Scholar." In *The Portable Emerson,* edited by Mark Van Doren, 23–46. New York: Viking Press, 1946.

Enzensberger, Hans Magnus. *The Consciousness Industry*. New York: Seabury, 1974.

Fiske, Edward B. *New York Times*, 5 Oct. 1988, sec. B12.

Fiske, John. *Television Culture*. New York: Methuen, 1987.

Flake, Carol. *Redemptorama: Culture, Politics and the New Evangelicism*. New York: Doubleday, 1984.

Frank, Waldo David. "Seriousness and Dada." *In The American Jungle*. New York: Farrar and Rinehart, 1937, 128–35.

Gedin, Per. *Literature in the Marketplace*. Translated by George Bisset. New York: Overlook Press, 1977.

Gobineau, Arthur. *Essay on the Inequality of Races*. In *Arthur Gobineau: Selected Political Writings*, ed. Michael D. Biddis. New York: Harper and Row, 1970.

Hawthorne, Nathaniel. *Twice-Told Tales*. Columbus: Ohio State Univ. Press, 1974.

Hey, Kenneth. "Marty: Aesthetics vs. Medium in Early Television Drama." *American History/American Television*. Edited by John E. O'Conner, 95–133. New York: Ungar, 1983.

Hoberman, J. *Vulgar Modernism*. Philadelphia: Temple Univ. Press, 1992.

Kammen, Michael. *Mystic Chords of Memory*. New York: Knopf, 1991.

Kerouac, Jack. *Good Blonde And Others*. Edited by Donald Allen. San Francisco: Grey Fox Press, 1993.

Lidz, Victor. "Television and Moral Order in a Secular Age." In *Media in Society: Readings in Mass Communication*, edited by Caren J. Deming and Samuel L. Becker, 53–69. Glenview, Ill.: Scott Foresman, 1988.

Lipsitz, George. "The Meaning of Memory: Family, Class and Ethnicity in Early Network Television Programs." *Cultural Anthropology* 1, no. 4 (Nov. 1986): 355–87.

———. *Time Passages: Collective Memory and American Popular Culture*. Minneapolis: Univ. of Minnesota Press, 1990.

Los Angeles Times, 12 Mar. 1988, sec. D2.

Macdonald, Dwight. "A Theory of Mass Culture." In *Mass Culture: The Popular Arts in America*, edited by Bernard Rosenberg and David M. White, 59–73. New York: Free Press, 1957.

MacDonald, J. Fred. *Television and the Red Menace: The Video Road to Vietnam*. New York: Praeger, 1985.

———. *Blacks and White TV: Afro-Americans In Television Since 1948*. Chicago: Nelson-Hall, 1983.

———. *Who Shot The Sheriff?: The Rise and Fall of the Television Western*. New York: Praeger, 1967.

McLuhan, Marshall. *Understanding Media: The Extensions of Man*. New York: Signet, 1964.

McNeil, Alex. *Total Television*. 2nd ed. New York: Penguin, 1984.

Mailer, Norman. *Advertisements for Myself*. New York: Perigree, 1976.

Marchand, Philip. *Marshall McLuhan: The Medium and the Messenger*. New York: Ticknor and Fields, 1989.

Marcuse, Herbert. *One-Dimensional Man*. Boston: Beacon Press, 1964.

Mehren, Elizabeth. "Test Scores Are Low, But What Do They Measure?" *Los Angeles Times*, 29 Sept. 1993, sec. E1.

Miller, Merle. "What It Means to Be a Homosexual." *New York Times Magazine*, 17 Jan. 1971, 9–11.

Newcomb, Horace. *TV: The Most Popular Art*. New York: /Doubleday, 1974.

Newcomb, Horace, and Alley, Robert S. *The Producer's Medium: Conversations with Creators of American TV*. New York: Oxford, 1983.

Ortega y Gasset, José. "The Coming of the Masses." In *The Revolt of the Masses* (1932). Reprinted in *Mass Culture: The Popular Arts in America*, edited by Bernard Rosenberg and David M. White, 41–45. New York: Free Press, 1957.

Paglia, Camille. *Sex, Art and American Culture*. New York: Vintage Books, 1992.

Paul, Sherman. *Repossessing and Renewing: The Green Tradition in American Culture*. Baton Rouge: Louisiana State Univ. Press, 1978.

Postman, Neil. *Amusing Ourselves to Death*. New York: Viking, 1985.

Rabinovitz, Lauren. "Television Criticism and American Studies." *American Quarterly* 43, no. 2 (June 1991): 358–70.

Rosenberg, Bernard, and White, David M., eds. *Mass Culture: The Popular Arts in America*. New York: Free Press, 1957.

Ross, Michael, and van den Haag, Ernest. *The Fabric of Society*. New York: Harcourt, Brace, 1957.

Schwarzbaum, Lisa. "Top Cops." *Entertainment Weekly* 29 Oct. 1993, 21.

Seldes, Gilbert. "The 'Errors' of Television." *Atlantic* May 1937, 531–41.

———. *The New Mass Media: Challenge to a Free Society*. Washington, D.C.: Public Affairs Press, 1968.

———. *The Public Arts*. New York: Simon and Schuster, 1956.

———. Review of *The Beverly Hillbillies*, *TV Guide* 15 Dec. 1962, 4.

———. *The Seven Lively Arts*. New York: Sagamore Press, 1924.

Sklar, Robert. *Movie-Made America: A Cultural History of American Movies*. New York: Random House, 1975.

Tocqueville, Alexis de. "In What Spirit the Americans Cultivate the Arts." *Democracy in America* (1835). Reprinted in *Mass Culture: The Popular Arts in America*, edited by Bernard Rosenberg and David M. White, 27–34. New York: Free Press, 1957.

Tumin, Melvin. "Popular Culture and the Open Society." In *Mass Culture: The Popular Arts in America*, edited by Bernard Rosenberg and David M. White, 548–56. New York: Free Press, 1957.

University of California Wellness Letter 9: 1 (Oct. 1992).

Vidal, Gore. *Live From Golgotha*. New York: Random House, 1992.

Warshow, Robert. *The Immediate Experience*. New York: Doubleday, 1962.

Watson, Mary Ann. *The Expanding Vista: American Television in the Kennedy Years*. New York: Oxford, 1990.

White, David Manning. "Mass Culture in America: Another Point of View." In *Mass Culture: The Popular Arts in America*, edited by Bernard Rosenberg and David M. White, 13–21. New York: Free Press, 1957.

Whitman, Walt. *The Complete Writings of Walt Whitman*. Edited by Richard M. Bucke, Thomas B. Harned, and Horace Traubel. New York: G. P. Putnam's Sons, 1902.

———. *Democratic Vistas and Other Papers*. London: Walter Scott, 1888.

———. *Leaves of Grass 1855*. Edited by Malcolm Cowley. New York: Penguin, 1976.

Index